DOUBLE TAKE
Two sides One story

CATHERINE CHARLEY

For Peter

This story is based, as much as possible, on primary source material - the words and pictures of the people that witnessed the events described. Whilst it is not possible to know the exact thoughts, feelings and motives of all the people involved, the book aims to give an insight into the experience of the events, based on the available evidence.

Scholastic Children's Books
Commonwealth House, 1–19 New Oxford Street,
London, WC1A 1NU, UK
A division of Scholastic Ltd
London ~ New York ~ Toronto ~ Sydney ~ Auckland
Mexico City ~ New Delhi ~ Hong Kong

Published in the UK by Scholastic Ltd, 2003

ISBN 0 439 98240 5

Printed and bound in Great Britain by Cox & Wyman,
Reading, Berkshire

Cover image supplied by: Alamy.com Limited. All rights reserved.

2 4 6 8 10 9 7 5 3 1

Contents

Prologue

RISK, EXCITEMENT, FEAR and danger – these words have all been used to describe a race that took place nearly 100 years ago – the race to be the first person ever to reach the South Pole. It was one of the toughest races in history, testing human endurance to its limits.

There were two teams – one Norwegian, the other British. The Norwegians were led by Roald Amundsen, the British by Robert Scott.

These men had never met but they were deadly rivals. They both wanted the glory of leading the first team of men across Antarctica to reach the South Pole. The Antarctic continent is a wild, dangerous and unforgiving place. Both teams of men encountered blizzards, gales and fog – not to mention sub-zero temperatures.

The race took place in the Antarctic summer months of October to March in 1911 – 1912. Even in the middle of summer near the South Pole the average temperatures range from −15 °C to −35 °C.

Amundsen intended to rely on dog sledges to take his supplies to the Pole. Scott planned to use not only dogs but also ponies, motor sledges and the men themselves. Scott and Amundsen knew their journeys were not going to be easy. They knew they had to cross mountains covered in frozen ice and snow to reach the high polar plateau where the Pole was believed to be. The teams had no radios and no means of contacting the outside world. Nor could they hope for rescue by aeroplane if they found themselves in life-threatening situations. Once they had landed on the continent and their supply ships had sailed off, they were on their own.

The Naval Officer

ROBERT FALCON SCOTT was born in 1868 near Plymouth in Devon, England. He was the third of five children, and the eldest boy. His family always knew him as "Con" – a shortened version of his second name.

Scott's father owned a brewery. He had a typical Victorian middle-class childhood with servants and a governess. At times he was considered a "sickly" child but, at 13, he joined the navy as an officer cadet and went to sea (as members of his family had been doing for generations).

Scott seems to have been popular with his fellow officers. They found he could be generous-hearted, sometimes absent-minded and, on occasion, hot-tempered. Scott was also described as *"a man of splendid physique"*. He was 5 feet 9 inches tall, with deep blue eyes, broad shoulders, a solid chest, and he was extremely fit.

Scott was in his twenties when his father was bankrupted, dying of a stroke three years later in 1897. Scott and his brother, Archie, now had to support their mother and two unmarried sisters. In 1898, his brother died of typhoid, leaving Scott as the main financial provider for his family. But his navy pay wasn't very high.

In the navy Scott had gradually moved up the ranks. However, after he reached the rank of Lieutenant, he knew that promotion could no longer be guaranteed – he would have to show that he deserved it. Scott was not sure he would gain promotion by merit at sea. But he knew there was another way – by commanding a polar expedition.

Since 1815 – after the wars with France had ended – the British navy had been involved in polar exploration. There had been several expeditions to the waters of both the Arctic and the Antarctic. One of the navy's main goals was to explore Antarctica – a continent about which almost nothing was known.

In 1887, while with the navy in the West Indies, Scott had a chance meeting with a man called Clements Markham. They met briefly again in 1896, when Scott was a torpedo officer on a ship off Spain. Now knighted, Sir Clements Markham had become President of the Royal Geographical Society (RGS), the great British expedition organization. Having been involved in polar exploration in his own naval days, Markham's obsession was to arrange a British expedition to Antarctica.

Three years later, when the RGS (in collaboration with the Royal Society of London) was seriously beginning to organize an Antarctic expedition, Scott was chosen to lead it. Scott's account states that he had bumped into Markham while walking down Buckingham Palace Road in London. Markham invited him to tea and told him about the expedition. Two days later Scott applied to lead it. No doubt Markham had a hand in encouraging him, feeling strongly that youth and stamina rather than experience were necessary to lead an expedition of this sort.

Scott was duly appointed and, after much preparation, the expedition left England in August 1901 in a specially built ship called *Discovery*. The aims of the expedition were twofold – to explore the new land and to carry out scientific work. There was no mention of reaching the South Pole.

The expedition sailed via New Zealand, reaching Antarctica in February 1902. Scott sailed into the Ross Sea and cruised along the 70-metre-high cliffs of the Ross Ice Shelf, a vast, floating piece of ice covering an area of 520,000 square kilometres – roughly the size of France. (James Clark Ross was a British naval commander who, in 1841, led the first expedition to reach the ice shelf, which now bears his name. He called it a "barrier" as it was blocking the way to the Pole. Scott and Amundsen, as all explorers of their time, referred to it simply as the "Barrier".)

Like all ice shelves, the Barrier is permanently attached to the landmass. Glaciers (rivers of ice) move across it towards the sea. Scott's men watched as large pieces of the ice shelf broke off, sending up enormous sprays of water, before floating northwards as massive icebergs.

Scott discovered land at the eastern end of the ice shelf, which he named King Edward VII Land – after the reigning British monarch. He then ordered his ship westwards to McMurdo Sound, a sea inlet that separates the Antarctic continent from Ross Island. (McMurdo Sound had also been discovered by Ross and he had named it after one of his officers.) Scott wanted to try and spend the winter there.

When the *Discovery* reached McMurdo Sound on 8 February 1902 Scott and his crew put out ice anchors in a small bay off the sound. On shore Scott arranged the erection of a prefabricated hut they had brought with them from Australia. They also put up two smaller huts nearby to house some of their scientific instruments. This spot became known as Hut Point.

It had been intended that the *Discovery* would return to New Zealand for the winter. Instead, Scott decided to let the ship freeze into the ice, using her as living quarters for everyone. He hoped that here, sheltered in the bay, she would be protected against the worst of the winter weather. He kept the large hut for emergencies in case the *Discovery* broke her moorings in a storm and was taken out to sea.

The days were getting shorter. The dark, sunless Antarctic winter was on its way. In Antarctica the sun disappears completely for about ten weeks of the year. Six months later, in the Antarctic mid-summer (December), the sun never falls below the horizon and daylight lasts 24 hours a day.

Scott organized some sledging activities before the sunlight faded for the winter. He wanted to test the equipment and to give the men some experience of travelling in extreme conditions: he had bought a number of huskies with him to try out and these dogs were divided into two teams.

Only one of the men on Scott's expedition had had any previous experience of dog-driving: the result was chaos. The dogs fought, got tangled up in the traces (harnesses), and at first refused to move at all. When one team did move, it bolted off completely out of control. There was much debate as to whether it was better to persuade the dogs to move with verbal encouragement or force them into action with whips.

When the first sledging group set out – a team of three men – it was decided not to use the dogs at all, but to pull the sledge themselves. So they harnessed themselves to the sledge to "man-haul" it. The men set off for White Island, about five or six miles to the south – or so they thought.

Although they took a tent, sleeping bags and food for three days with them, they believed the trip out would take only an afternoon. But it took them two days to get there. In this part of the world shape and distance can be deceptive and distant objects are often much further away than they appear to the naked eye. When the men got caught in a blizzard, their feet began to sweat, causing ice to form in their boots. They were so exhausted by struggling through the storm that they had hardly any energy to put up the tent and cook their food. They hadn't met the worst Antarctic conditions by any means, but they had nearly died.

Skiing was another new experience for most of the men. Scott encouraged them to practise. He wrote, *"Figure after figure can be seen flying down the hillside, all struggling hard to keep their balance."*

Another sledging test trip involved four officers, eight men and four sledges (Scott had intended to accompany them but he had injured his knee skiing). The team made their way to Cape Crozier to build a cairn (a mound made of stones). They would place directions to the expedition's winter quarters in the cairn. They took the dogs, but they kept fighting so the men man-hauled the loaded sledges. On the return journey they found themselves making their way through a terrible blizzard. One man died when he fell over a cliff into the sea and the others were lucky to make it to safety.

Scott organized one further short expedition before the winter really set in. He wanted to gain experience of sledging, and he wished to give the opportunity to as many of the others as possible. His aim was to set out supply depots of food and fuel going southwards; these were to be used by the spring sledging parties on the way back from their expeditions so they could carry less weight with them as they explored. He set off with three officers, eight men, three sledges, nine dogs and supplies for three weeks. The dogs proved very difficult to work with; some even had to be dragged along in their traces. After three days, in the face of these difficulties and with the temperatures falling as low as –44 °C, the expedition was abandoned and the team returned to base.

On 23 April 1902 the sun disappeared and the men spent the next four months in the dark Antarctic winter. They lived on the ship (which was now locked in the ice) using the prefabricated hut for recreational activities – such as putting on plays.

Scott organized the expedition team to carry out many scientific experiments over the winter months. The experiments included taking readings of temperature and wind speed every two hours, a hazardous task in blizzards with temperatures dropping to –40 °C. The scientists also measured the tides with an instrument invented by Scott and made by the expedition engineer. Further readings were taken to record the Earth's magnetic pull, using delicate instruments brought for the purpose from Germany. Other men caught marine plants in traps through holes in the ice, so they could analyse them.

One of the scientists, Dr Edward Wilson (known as "Uncle Bill" by the men), caught and dissected penguins and carried out other experiments on them. They were kept frozen until they were needed, when Wilson would put them on the shelf above the stove to defrost. He was also a fine artist and sketched many of the scenes in Antarctica, often by moonlight.

When September brought the Antarctic spring, Scott sent out more sledging parties. Learning from earlier experiences, the sledges were now packed so that the loads were less likely to shift as they were pulled along. Small teams were sent to carry out surveys of the surrounding area, but often they found their clothing totally inadequate against the cold, wild winds and blizzards.

The men wore many layers of tweed, wool and cotton including woollen pullovers, thick socks and tweed jackets. Over the top they wore windproof jackets and trousers of very finely woven cotton. All these were warm fabrics, but the outfits were tight at the wrists and ankles, trapping sweat and not allowing it to dry off. A man hauling a sledge generated a great deal of sweat and, in conditions such as these, the sweat could turn to ice, making it difficult for the men to move their bodies properly. Then it could melt again leaving the clothes damp, possibly leading to hypothermia – where the body loses heat faster than it can produce it. Someone can switch from being very cold to dangerously cold very quickly – often because of a mixture of wind, wet clothes, tiredness and hunger.

On their heads, under their waterproof hoods, the men wore a variety of woollen hats and wrapped felt scarves round their necks. But, as their hoods were not attached to their jackets, precious body heat was lost.

They wore wolfskin mittens and reindeer-fur boots – the same as those worn by the native peoples of the Arctic; these were lined with a special grass to absorb sweat. Unfortunately, these often began to moult as they wore out.

C

On 2 November 1902, Scott, Wilson and Second Lieutenant Ernest Shackleton (an officer in the Merchant Navy) set off on the key journey of the expedition; they aimed to travel southwards towards the Pole to see how far they could get. This was to take the men over territory no one had ever crossed before. They left with a large supporting party to help carry supplies along the route. There were five sledges and all 19 of the dogs. Scott never expressed a hope of getting to the Pole on this trip, though Wilson wrote:

> *Our object is to get as far south in a straight line on the Barrier as we can, reach the Pole if possible, or find some new land, anyhow do all we can in the time and get back to the ship at the end of January.*

Any adventurer to an unknown land pinpoints their position using imaginary lines called latitude and longitude. Geographers use these lines to divide up the surface of the world into a grid. If an explorer can measure his latitude and longitude he can find his position on the grid and, therefore, his exact position on the globe.

Lines of latitude give distances in degrees (°) north and south of the Equator, the imaginary line that runs round the middle of the Earth. So 1° North is just above the Equator and 1° South is just south of it. The North Pole is 90° North and the South Pole is 90° South. Lines of longitude give distances in degrees east and west of the Prime Meridian (also known as the Greenwich Meridian), the imaginary line running from pole to pole (all lines of longitude meet at the poles). Degrees of latitude and longitude are subdivided into minutes (') – with 60 minutes to each degree. For example, the position of London is written: 51° 30' North (of the Equator) and 00° 05' West (of the Prime Meridian). A minute is equal to one nautical mile.

This book will refer to distances in nautical miles, as Scott and Amundsen did. A nautical mile is equivalent to 1.15 land miles or 1.85 kilometres.

For Antarctic explorers lines of latitude were particularly important: they showed how far southwards they had travelled, and there are few distinguishing features to help measure distance in any other way on the trackless wastes of the continent.

When Scott's large southern party reached 79° South (11 degrees from the Pole – or 660 nautical miles), he ordered half of the support team to turn back. Two days later, on 15 November 1902, Scott told the rest of the supply team to return to base, leaving him with two companions, Shackleton and Wilson, to continue southwards alone.

But the very next day the dogs seemed to lose heart and would hardly pull. As the days wore on they became thinner and thinner. The men tied themselves to the sledges and helped the huskies to haul. If a dog died it was fed to the others and an improvement was noted. Eventually, if a dog was too weak to continue, it was shot. The diaries of all three men express their regret at these deaths. For example Scott wrote: *"Poor old Grannie pulled till she could pull no longer and lay down in the snow; they put her on a sledge and she soon died."*

Scott decided to turn back on 31 December 1902. He had reached a latitude of 82° 17' South. This was still about 480 miles from the Pole, but it was over 227 miles further south than anyone had ever been before. To the south they noted a distant range of high mountains (later to be named the Transantarctic Mountains) lying across their route.

On the return journey Scott decided, to the relief of all, that they should untie the remaining dogs and let them follow the sledge freely. Scott wrote:

> *No more cheering and dragging in front, no more shouting and yelling behind, no more clearing of tangled traces, no more dismal stoppages, and no more whip.*

Scott added that he would prefer ten days of man-hauling to one spent in driving a worn-out dog team. Now, instead of shouting at the animals, the men spent the time talking to each other and found that each day's tough journey seemed to pass more quickly. However, relations between Scott and Shackleton had become strained during the course of the trip and a mutual dislike began to emerge. They quarrelled because Shackleton did not agree with many of Scott's decisions.

The expedition was plagued by health problems, too. Wilson had horrible attacks of snow-blindness. Snow-blindness can be caused by the bright glare off snow and ice. The eyes are temporarily damaged and become very itchy, feeling as though they are full of grit. The sufferer gets terrible headaches and, in extreme cases, loss of vision. Even in overcast conditions in polar regions, goggles should be worn to protect the eyes. Wilson was in the habit of taking his off while sketching so that he could view the scene more clearly. On one occasion his blindness was so bad that he had to spend a day pulling the sledge blindfolded, while Scott guided him verbally.

Far more serious, however, were the signs of scurvy that Wilson had found when examining Shackleton. One of the first signs is bleeding gums, which become swollen, blackened and spongy. Other signs include teeth becoming loose and falling out; arms and legs feeling very stiff, painful and swollen; sores on the skin; and wounds not healing. If untreated the symptoms become worse and worse until the person dies. In Scott's time no one knew what caused scurvy. It was not until the 1920s that it was discovered that scurvy is caused by a lack of Vitamin C, which is found in fresh food, especially fruit and vegetables, as well as fresh meat.

Scott, like all explorers of his time, had been trying to prevent the disease among his men and believed, correctly, that eating seal meat could help prevent it. At the base camp, he had tried to persuade his men to eat more seal meat. Despite this, Shackleton was steadily getting weaker. He could no longer help pull the sledge and had to walk beside it. Scott and Wilson kept going on their skis, man-hauling the sledge between them.

Meanwhile, the three men endured hostile weather conditions. There could be "white-outs" for several days at a time. White-outs occur when the sky is overcast. There are no shadows so perspective is lost, the ground blurs into the sky and the horizon disappears: everything takes on the same uniform shade of white or grey. What appears to be a flat area could be a dip, or a big hill could look like a little bump. This optical illusion makes it easy to lose your way. In such conditions even birds can get disorientated and lose their sense of perspective, sometimes flying straight into the ground. *"One cannot see one's own footsteps in soft snow in this light,"* wrote Wilson during this trek. Scott wrote, *"It is difficult to describe the trying nature of this work, for hours one plods on, ever searching for some definite sign."*

Increasingly exhausted, the men struggled on. Their food began to run out, and Scott and Wilson started to suffer from scurvy, too. But, on 18 January 1903, they reached a supply depot – just 60 miles from the ship. The extra food helped them all. Even Shackleton improved; yet he still could not haul, often felt dizzy and was continuing to cough up spots of blood. When at last the men got back to Hut Point, Scott sent Shackleton home on the relief ship.

The three-man team had been away for 93 days and had covered 960 miles. Scott concluded, *"If we had not achieved such great results as we had hoped for we knew at least that we had striven and endured with all our might."*

They had surveyed 300 miles and added to knowledge of the Barrier. Scott and his men had got nearer to the South Pole than any one else. It was no small achievement.

C

Scott spent another year in Antarctica, supervizing scientific tasks over the winter months and carrying out more exploratory expeditions the following spring. In February 1904 he left Antarctica on the *Discovery* and returned to England.

Back home Scott was welcomed as a great "Antarctic hero" and was promoted to the rank of Captain by the navy. He undertook a round of dinners and lectures and wrote a book about the expedition called *The Voyage of the Discovery*. He met and married his wife, Kathleen Bruce, an independent artist and sculptress – a very modern woman for her time. It is rumoured that Kathleen married Scott simply because she liked the idea of being married to a famous polar explorer!

Two years after Scott returned to England, Shackleton organized his own expedition to Antarctica –

this time to try to reach the South Pole. Scott told Shackleton, among other things, that he was not to use "his" base – McMurdo Sound. Shackleton agreed to use the Bay of Whales, an indent in the ice shelf and natural harbour, as his base. Unfortunately, when Shackleton arrived in Antarctica, he had no other option than to use McMurdo because ice blocked his way to the Bay of Whales. When Scott discovered this he was thrown into a state of rage. He is said never to have forgiven Shackleton.

Shackleton's polar expedition of 1907–1909 followed the route that he, Scott and Wilson had pioneered, this time using ponies to transport supplies to the foot of the Transantarctic Mountains. Then Shackleton took his men on up the Beardmore Glacier (which he named after one of his sponsors, a rich Glasgow businessman), man-hauling everything they needed behind them. On 9 January 1909 they reached latitude 88° 23' South. They could probably have completed the 100 miles left to the Pole, but they might never have made it home because their supplies were running short. So Shackleton turned back, bringing all his men to safety.

Shackleton's epic trip was highly praised when he got back to England and he was knighted. Scott was very resentful of Sir Ernest's success and popularity, seeing him as a dangerous rival to his own fame. Scott felt his own position in polar exploration needed to be proved. He had to get to the South Pole himself – not only before another British man, but before anyone else!

Ironically, when Scott returned to England after his first expedition to Antarctica, he had written privately, *"Wherever my destiny may in future lead me, I hope it will not be to the interior of the Antarctic continent."* But Shackleton's attempt had changed his mind.

While Shackleton was away, Scott – with the enthusiastic support of his wife, Kathleen – started to plan a new expedition to the Antarctic. He announced it in *The Times* in September 1909, just a few days after his son, Peter, was born.

The RGS was not as supportive as Scott had expected, nor were other potential major sponsors. There were other, more serious things to worry about. There was talk of war with Germany. Not many people were keen on putting money into an expedition. Scott raised some money – including £20,000 from the government (they had given Shackleton the same) – but by no means enough.

However, Scott was not wholly unsuccessful – he had enlisted on to his team an energetic 28-year-old naval lieutenant, Edward (Teddy) Evans. Lieutenant Evans had been planning to organize his own expedition to Antarctica and had already raised some money. In return for his support and his funds, Scott promised Evans the position of Second-in-Command.

This time Scott couldn't afford to have a new boat specially built. He tried to buy back the *Discovery* but the owners wouldn't sell her. An old Scottish whaler, the *Terra Nova*, was obtained instead and prepared for the voyage.

Scott began to recruit men and get stores and supplies ready. Over 8,000 applied to join, including several of his team from the *Discovery* expedition. His great friend Dr Wilson was now to be Chief of Scientific Staff. He also recruited some of the *Discovery* seamen, including the tough and dependable William Lashley, the Irish "giant" Thomas Crean, and Petty Officer Edgar "Taff" Evans, a large Welshman full of energy, humour and resourcefulness.

Among the others were two rich young men who each paid at least £1,000 into the expedition's coffers when they joined up. One was an army officer, Captain Lawrence "Titus" Oates, who had fought in the Boer War in South Africa nearly a decade before. Oates had been in the cavalry and knew a great deal about horses and ponies. The other was Apsley Cherry-Garrard, an intelligent young man who had just left Oxford University and who was recruited as Assistant Zoologist on the recommendation of Wilson.

Scott made arrangements for the expedition to carry out scientific studies into many facets of Antarctica, including geographical, geological, meteorological and biological surveys. Although the primary aim of Scott's expedition was to reach the South Pole, there was also going to be a large scientific team on board and there were plans, too, to send a second expedition to explore King Edward VII Land.

Scott sent Cecil Meares, his dog expert, to Russia and Siberia to buy the dogs and ponies he wanted for the expedition. Meares had been a fur-trader in this area and had experience of dog-driving so chose the dogs well. Although Scott had decided to take some dogs to help pull supply sledges, he certainly did not want to rely on them totally – they had not proved particularly successful on the *Discovery* expedition and Shackleton had not had much success with them either. Additionally, Scott did not believe that dogs could pull sledges up mountains. He knew that he was going to have to climb up the Beardmore Glacier (along Shackleton's route) to reach the Pole so he decided that the dogs were going to be used only to carry supplies as far as the foot of the glacier.

This time Scott's aim was to use mainly ponies to pull the sledges. Ponies had proved useful for Shackleton in pulling large loads and Scott thought that Siberian ponies would be well used to ice and snow. After a close reading of Shackleton's book on the 1907–1909 expedition, he noted that the white ponies seemed to be stronger and last longer. Meares was ordered to buy white ones if possible. (Actually, the fact that the white ponies survived better on Shackleton's expedition seems just to have been coincidence.)

As well as dogs and ponies Scott had a brand-new invention to take with him – the motor sledge. (These were forerunners of *Sno-Cats* which were used in the first successful crossing of the Antarctic continent in the 1950s by Sir Edmund Hillary and Sir Vivian Fuchs.)

Three motor sledges were ordered for the expedition and Scott had high hopes for them. They could pull much heavier and larger loads than either dogs or ponies. Scott went to Norway to test them out and the results were encouraging.

Despite the shortage of funds, by the summer of 1910 the *Terra Nova* was fully equipped. She sailed from Britain amid a lot of publicity and excitement. Scott was setting out to beat Shackleton's record. He felt the South Pole was his right. He said, *"What matters now is that the Pole should be obtained by an Englishman."*

Little did Scott know that Shackleton was not to be his only rival in Antarctica...

Amundsen
Plans for the North Pole
1872 – 1910

ROALD ENGEBRETH GRAVNING Amundsen was born on 16 July 1872, a few years later than Scott. He was the fourth of four boys and was brought up on the edge of Christiania (now Oslo in Norway, which was then part of Sweden).

Amundsen came from a reasonably wealthy middle-class background. His father's family was involved in shipping and he had been brought up around boats. Like most Norwegian children he quickly became skilled at cross-country skiing. He had put on his first pair of skis almost as soon as he could walk. From an early age, he had always wanted to explore and, in his teens, he had developed a firm desire to go to the North Pole.

But Amundsen's mother had different ideas for her son (his father had died when he was 14). She wanted him to become a doctor, so he went to medical school until he was 21. When his mother died in 1893 Amundsen left and started to follow his own ambitions.

By now Amundsen was over six-feet tall with fair hair, sharp features and piercing blue eyes. He was physically very fit and always very single-minded when he had set his heart on something. He was hard-working and serious. He was also short-sighted, a fact he always tried to hide, seldom wearing his glasses.

Amundsen's ultimate aim was to reach the North Pole. He became involved in various activities in preparation, including many long skiing trips with friends in the Norwegian mountains. Using his family connections in shipping he found work on a whaling ship in Arctic waters where he learned navigation skills and gained his Mate's Certificate.

In 1896 Amundsen applied for a place on a Belgian expedition to the Antarctic, on a ship called the *Belgica*, and was offered the position of Second Mate. This was his first experience of polar exploration.

The *Belgica* sailed south the following year and, by accident, became the first ship ever to overwinter in Antarctica. The Captain, Adrien de Gerlache, had planned to land a few men on Cape Adare – at the end of Victoria Land (on the edge of the Ross Sea) – and then to send the ship to safety before the pack ice closed in. But on 2 March the *Belgica* became trapped. Pack ice is an area of sea that is densely packed with ice floes. These floes move around with the winds and currents and crash together in rough, stormy seas, often getting pushed on top of each other. It is possible for a ship to make her way through the channels of water between ice floes but as winter approaches the floes can freeze together, trapping and even crushing a vessel.

The *Belgica* found herself locked in the ice for more than a year. During the winter months there was no sun at all. On board there were full sets of winter clothing for only four people and spirits became very low: two members of the crew went mad and many feared they were doomed never to escape alive. There was also a severe outbreak of scurvy on board. The ship's American doctor, Dr Frederick Cook, thought that seal meat should be eaten to keep scurvy at bay. Thankfully some men were persuaded to do this and the situation improved.

Amundsen watched and noted everything, learning a great deal. From the very beginning of the trip he had been writing all his thoughts into his diary. It became full of tips on polar exploration.

In late January 1898, he had taken part in the first ever sledging journey and overnight camp in Antarctica itself, on an ice-covered island off Graham Land (now known as the Antarctic Peninsula, a massive piece of land jutting out into the sea towards South America – east of the Ross Ice Shelf). On this trip the group had man-hauled their sledges over a steep ice-slope pitted with treacherous crevasses.

A crevasse is a deep, and often seemingly bottomless, crack in the ice. It can be anything from a few millimetres wide to 30 metres or more across. Antarctic explorers have talked about some that are big enough to swallow up a whole ship! A crevasse occurs when the ice splits and breaks apart as it moves over hidden rocks or downhill, often in glaciers. The greatest danger comes when a crevasse is concealed by snow – known as a "lidded" crevasse. Sometimes, snow can form a bridge over an open crevasse which provides a useful crossing point – but only if the snow is strong enough to take the weight of the person. If the explorer also has a sledge of heavy supplies and equipment the danger of falling in increases.

It wasn't only crevasses that were a problem for Amundsen on this sledging trip. He, like the others, found man-hauling heavy, tiring work. He felt it was a stupid way to move supplies if there were better alternatives. Amundsen made further notes in his journal – snow goggles were *"absolutely necessary"*; the tent could be a better shape against the wind; sealskin clothing such as that worn by Dr Cook (himself an experienced Arctic explorer) was warmer, more practical and dried better.

Amundsen's time on the *Belgica* was a great learning experience for him, but during the long months stuck in the ice Amundsen had quarrelled with the captain and resigned his post. When the *Belgica* was eventually released from the pack ice in March 1899 Amundsen left the ship as soon as he could – when she reached South America.

Once back in Norway Amundsen started to organize his own polar expedition – a trip to take the first ship through the whole of the North-West Passage – the sea-route around the top of North America. This would be a historic polar first. He also decided to make for the North Magnetic Pole on the same trip. The Magnetic Poles are different from the Geographical Poles. While the Geographical Poles are fixed at one place – where the lines of longitude meet at the top and bottom of the globe (see page 15) – the Magnetic Poles are always drifting, moving slowly about 10–15 kilometres per year due to the effect of the Earth's orbit around the sun. Magnetic compasses always line up with the Magnetic Poles.

Amundsen bought a small wooden boat, the *Gjøa*, and took her on a trial five-month voyage into the Arctic Ocean – with her former skipper as his Mate (to give Amundsen the best possible tuition) and with sealers as his crew. They were to catch seals to pay for the cost of the trip. On this journey Amundsen also wanted to see if it was possible to survive on a long journey mainly on seal meat, and to see if it really did help prevent scurvy.

He also used this time to study the effectiveness of pemmican as food. Pemmican is a mix of dried meat mixed with melted fat. It was already in use as a sledging ration by polar explorers. Before modern dehydrated food it was the most nourishing form of concentrated food available. Amundsen decided to make his own for the North-West Passage expedition, thinking it would be better than any bought preprepared.

It was on this trial trip that he began to make contacts with the Lapps, people living in the Arctic conditions of northern Scandinavia. From them he bought excellent reindeer furs and clothes that were not usually available to commercial buyers, as well as sleeping bags and *finnesko* (soft reindeer fur) boots. The Arctic peoples usually kept the best furs for themselves but Amundsen managed to persuade them to sell some to him.

He also observed that dog sledges were the main form of transport over the snow and ice for the people who lived there. He decided that this would be the best way to reach the North Magnetic Pole from the ship during his planned expedition. But he had no experience of dog-driving, it was not a Norwegian mode of transport – so he began to learn.

On his return from the trial voyage, he gathered together a small, carefully chosen team of six for the polar expedition. Among them were Adolf Lindstrøm (as cook) and Helmer Hanssen – both men who were later to be part of his team as he raced for the South Pole against Scott.

The *Gjøa* trip took three years (1903–1906). She was the first boat to complete the whole journey through the North-West Passage. When the sea froze over in the winter months Amundsen allowed her to be trapped by the ice. He then waited until the sea thawed in the spring to continue the journey. During the expedition Amundsen met many Inuit people and learned much about how the native peoples of the Arctic travelled. He also learned how they handled and used their husky dogs, and how they made their clothes. And, as planned, he reached the North Magnetic Pole by dog sledge.

With the success of this first voyage through the North-West Passage Amundsen became a celebrated polar explorer. He immediately started planning for his next goal – to be the first to reach the North Pole; his dream since his teens.

Amundsen decided that the best way to achieve this was to allow his ship to be frozen into the Arctic ice and to drift with the ocean current across the Pole itself. Unlike Antarctica, which is a continent, the Arctic is a frozen sea and its ice moves with the tides and currents below it. From studying where the remains of some former shipwrecks had ended up, Amundsen had worked out that the currents in the sea below would probably carry the ice – and thus the ship – near, if not over, the Pole.

Amundsen asked the great Norwegian Arctic explorer, Nansen, for help. Nansen was world famous. In the mid-1890s, he and fellow Norwegian, Hjalmar Johansen, left their ship, the *Fram*, and set off over the Arctic ice with dog sledges and kayaks for the North Pole – a journey they had assumed would take four or five months. But it was to be a year-and-a-half before they reached safety. The Arctic ice had thawed as summer arrived and they had been forced to canoe to remote Arctic islands to escape death.

Amundsen asked if he could borrow Nansen's old ship, the *Fram* (meaning "forward" in Norwegian), which had been specially built for polar travel. She was a very wide ship – nearly a third wide as she was long (10 metres wide by 36 metres long) – and had a rounded hull. Nansen had proved, on expedition, that this shape of hull was lifted up rather than crushed when the pack ice closed in on her. She also had a modern diesel engine so she started much more quickly than the other ships of the time that had coal-fired steam engines.

Amundsen's plans were well underway for his proposed drift to the North Pole when, in September 1909, the news came through that not just one expedition, but two, claimed to have reached it! They were both American – Robert E Peary said he had travelled there overland from Greenland on 6 April 1909. The other expedition leader was Amundsen's old companion from the *Belgica*, Dr Frederick Cook. He claimed that he had got there a full year before Peary on 21 April 1908, also overland. A row ensued over who had got there first, and many accused Cook of never having been there at all.

Neither Cook nor Peary provided enough information on navigational observations from their journeys to prove their stories. (Today many people doubt that either of them actually reached the North Pole – the first person who, without doubt, stood at the North Pole was Gordiyenko from the Soviet Union who landed there in a plane in 1948.) But it didn't matter to Amundsen which one had got to the North Pole first – his life-long dream had been shattered. What was he to do now?

He decided to turn his attentions southwards.

Amundsen knew that Scott was preparing for a trip to Antarctica so he decided to tell only a few people about his own revised plans. He thought it was best to keep quiet, fearing that if he made his change of plan public Scott would get a lot more support, and therefore money, in England. He also feared that Nansen would not let him take the *Fram* across the oceans of the world to Antarctica. Amundsen continued with his preparations as if he was still aiming to go to the North Pole, but he made small, secret changes.

Amundsen gathered dogs and sledges for his expedition. He hand-picked a small team, which included Hjalmar Johansen, Nansen's companion in his epic Arctic journey of 1893–1896. Like Amundsen the men all had experience of ice and snow and most had undertaken years of skiing and sledge-driving activities in the snowy lands of their native Norway and other parts of the Arctic. They all believed they were going north into the Arctic Circle.

On 7 June 1910 Amundsen and his team sailed from Norway – quietly and under cover of darkness as he didn't want to have to answer questions from journalists – and set his ship's course southwards. It didn't appear strange to set off south for a trip to the northernmost part of the Earth. For the *Fram* to start from the west of North America to try to drift with the currents to the North Pole, she had to sail round half the world to get there – south from Europe through the Atlantic Ocean, around Cape Horn at the bottom of South America and then northwards again.

It was only in September when Amundsen reached Madeira (an island off the coast of west Africa), that he told his shocked crew that he was planning to sail south to make for Antarctica instead of going north. He gave each man the option of leaving but they all decided to stay with him. He now had to let the world know of his change of plans. He did this by sending off various cables. One of these was to the King of Norway, Haakon VII. Another, sent on 9 September 1910, was to Scott, his rival:

> BEG LEAVE TO INFORM YOU PROCEEDING
> ANTARCTICA. AMUNDSEN.

Scott received Amundsen's telegram when he reached Melbourne, Australia on 12 October 1910.

The race was on …

The *Terra Nova*

October 1910 – January 1911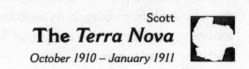

SCOTT WAS LITERALLY dumbstruck when he read Amundsen's telegram. He kept quiet about it for several days and told only one member of his team, swearing him to secrecy. He wasn't even certain that Amundsen's telegram meant that the Norwegian was going for the Pole itself. He must have hoped against hope that he wasn't.

Scott made his first public announcement on the possibility of a race with Amundsen on 27 October in Wellington, New Zealand. He was interviewed by a local journalist and asked to comment on the rumour, now in all the papers, that Amundsen was challenging him for the Pole. He replied, *"If Amundsen wants to try for the South Pole, I can only wish him good luck."*

But Scott wasn't as relaxed about the prospect of a race as he appeared to be. Publicly he pretended to be calm, but privately he was furious. He felt that Amundsen had acted very badly in keeping quiet about the real intentions of his own expedition for so long.

In front of his men Scott scoffed at the large number of dogs Amundsen was bringing to Antarctica. He told his expedition members that with motor sledges, ponies and their willingness to man-haul they would be able to beat the Norwegian's dog teams and reach the South Pole first.

Scott spent the next month in New Zealand organizing further supplies for the *Terra Nova*. Meanwhile the *Terra Nova* was put into dry dock to repair a leak that had been apparent on the trip south. The next part of her voyage would involve crossing the Southern Ocean, the roughest sea in the world. It was no place for serious leaks.

The stores were rearranged and repacked so that everything was marked – red for the main polar team, and green for the eastern team (which was to go with Lieutenant Victor Campbell to explore King Edward VII Land). The scientific instruments were checked. There was a trial run to put up the prefabricated expedition hut. It was made of wood and was 14.6 metres long and 7.3 metres wide. The walls were going to be insulated with seaweed sown into sacks.

The ship was then loaded up. Stalls had been built for the 19 ponies that had joined the expedition here – taking over some of the crew's quarters. Unfortunately, it was now discovered that Meares knew little about ponies. Meares is reported to have said that the seller in Siberia had gone away with a smile on his face when he was given the money! Captain Oates, Scott's horse expert, was horrified by the state of the animals when he saw them for the first time in New Zealand. They were all quite old and four of them were lame. Oates was to care for them during the course of the expedition.

Meares did redeem himself, however, when it came to choosing sledge dogs. The 33 dogs he had brought out to New Zealand were fit and healthy and suitable for the job. For the voyage to Antarctica the dogs were chained on to the cramped deck of the *Terra Nova*.

Many of the provisions put into the ship in New Zealand were food supplies for the animals and men. Oates argued for 45 tonnes of pony food to be loaded on board (and loaded another two tonnes at his own expense without Scott knowing). There were five tonnes of dog food. The supplies taken on board for the men included 162 carcasses of mutton.

There were endless other items wedged in wherever possible – sledges, warm clothing, scientific equipment, a machine to provide gas to light the hut, and the hut itself. Not to mention nearly 500 tonnes of coal for the ship's engine! The three motor sledges, which were still in their crates, were lashed to the deck. In addition to all this there were 65 men. The poor *Terra Nova* was not made for carrying this kind of load. She was very overcrowded and many of the crew shared hammocks. When one went on watch another took his place in the hammock. This overloading made the ship very unstable.

Nevertheless, on 29 November the ship set sail for Antarctica. Her final berth had been in Port Chalmers and the town declared a local holiday when she left. Crowds cheered as the *Terra Nova* steamed away from New Zealand's shores.

C

Three days later the *Terra Nova* found herself in the middle of a terrible storm, tossed about by the enormous waves of the wildest sea in the world – the Southern Ocean. Some of the cargo on the deck was dislodged, making the ship even more unstable. The winds howled at gale force ten, as waves – often more than ten-metres high – broke across the deck. The ponies were thrown against the sides of their stalls while the ship lurched around in the furious seas and water lashed the poor dogs chained up on the decks. The men and animals feared for their lives.

As she tossed violently, the overloaded *Terra Nova* took on more water in the storm than she might have done with less cargo. Older planks on the deck broke under the weight of the waves. Water washed down into the cabins and the engine room. The pumps strained hard to get the water out. But then they stopped, clogged up with a watery mix of engine oil and coal dust.

At once the water level began to rise inside the ship and started to lap at the coal fires that kept the steam engine going. The fires went out and the engine stopped. Now without power, the *Terra Nova* was left to the mercy of the sea.

As an experienced naval man, Scott remained calm. Bowers later wrote that "*Captain Scott was simply splendid*." With his Second-in-Command, Lieutenant Evans, he arranged the men into teams to bail out the water by hand throughout the night.

Wilson wrote:

> *It was a weird night's work with the howling gale and the darkness and the immense sea running over the ship every few minutes, and no engine and no sail, and we all in the engine room black as ink with engine-room oil and bilgewater, singing shanties as we passed up slopping buckets full of bilge, each man above slopping a little over the heads of all of us below him, wet through to the skin...*

After 12 hours of working in water up to their necks, Lieutenant Evans, the Chief Engineer and the ship's carpenter, managed to reach the valve of the hand pump and clear the oily blockage. This enabled the rest of the crew to bring the flooding under control.

This terrifying ordeal went on for a day and a half, but finally the storm began to abate. All the men were safe. But they had lost two ponies, 10 tonnes of coal, 300 litres of petrol and one dog. Incredibly, another dog had been swept off the ship by one wave but thrown back on to deck by another.

On 8 December, as the *Terra Nova* got nearer to Antarctica, the first iceberg was spotted. The following day she reached the pack ice. Over the next three weeks the ice floes slowed her down severely. Using all her strength the ship had to push and force her way slowly through the floating ice, using up a lot of precious coal as she did so.

But the slowness of their progress gave Scott the opportunity to organize skiing lessons for his men on one of the larger ice floes. He had brought with him a skiing instructor, Tryggve ("Trigger") Gran, a Norwegian, and an impromptu ski school was set up. Scott let the men choose whether they wanted to learn to ski. Most of the officers and scientists attempted to learn, but the rest of the crew weren't keen to try. Those that did were soon having a lot of fun hurtling around on their skis.

◘

At the beginning of January the crew spotted the volcano, Mount Erebus. Everyone looked out in awe at the majestic view. At 3,795 metres high this is the larger of Ross Island's two volcanoes and the most southerly active volcano in the world.

Now that he had reached the landmass of the continent Scott had to find somewhere to unload – and to set up his winter base. He had hoped to land at the old *Discovery* headquarters at Hut Point – on the tip of Ross Island, by McMurdo Sound – and use this base again. However, he found his way blocked by frozen seas so he decided to set up his base six miles further along the coast of the island, on a headland that he named Cape Evans after his Second-in-Command. It was 4 January 1911.

Even here, about a mile-and-a-half of solid ice lay between the shore and the open sea. The *Terra Nova* anchored to this ice and unloading began. As soon as the ponies reached firm ground they rolled in the snow and kicked about, happy to be off the swaying boat.

All the equipment had to be taken over the ice to the shore, a job that was to take two weeks. Scott used his various different modes of transport to do this – ponies, dogs, motor sledges and manpower. Unfortunately, during the unloading process the largest motor sledge, which was being pulled by 20 men, fell through the ice into the depths of the sea below. Scott now had only two motor sledges to help him get to the Pole. But the remaining vehicles proved extremely useful in hauling heavy quantities of stores across the ice. They could drag more weight than the men, dogs or the ponies. Scott still hoped they were going to be his big advantage in the race to the Pole.

While unloading took place, the prefabricated base camp hut was assembled on the beach at Cape Evans, on the shore of McMurdo Sound – "Home Beach", Scott called it. Twenty-five men were going to overwinter there. Cape Evans was 77° 38' South, about 750 miles from the Pole. Within two weeks of their arrival the hut was built and on 18 January the men took up residence.

With unloading completed, Scott sent the *Terra Nova* off eastwards, along the Ross Ice Shelf, to King Edward VII Land to find somewhere for Lieutenant Campbell and his Eastern Party to overwinter. This six-man group aimed to explore King Edward VII Land in the spring while Scott's Southern Party was making for the Pole. However, finding that heavy ice prevented them getting near to King Edward VII Land, Campbell decided to enter the Bay of Whales to see if the team could be landed there. But what they found was another ship at anchor.

Amundsen
The *Fram*
September 1910 – February 1911

AFTER HIS SHIP, the *Fram*, had left Madeira, Amundsen could work openly on his preparations for the expedition to the South Pole. He was a great planner and as he sailed south he worked out his schedule in minute detail.

Amundsen put up a map of the Antarctic with a summary of his plans in the chartroom. He gathered his men together and told them that his sole aim was to lead the first team of men ever to reach the South Pole and to beat the British there. And then – this was just as important, he felt – he wanted to be the first to get the news back to the world's press.

Amundsen's plan was to land in the Bay of Whales and to set up his winter base there. He wanted to lay some depots along the beginning of his route to the Pole before winter set in. After overwintering at the base he would lead his team to the Pole and then return to the Bay of

Whales as quickly as possible. He hoped that he and his team would be able to board the *Fram* as soon as she arrived back after wintering in South America where she would carry out a survey of the Southern Ocean. Then he planned to return to a cable station in Tasmania, off Australia, to tell the world the news.

Amundsen had great confidence in the dogs he had brought with him, specially chosen from northern Greenland. Huskies were used to pulling loaded sledges on long journeys at speed over snow and ice. And, most importantly, they were able to stay outside at night with no extra shelter built for them. The dogs could curl themselves up into a snow-hole and remain warm, as they sweated through their tongues, not their coats. The dogs were Amundsen's main priority on the voyage south. The animals were well looked after as Amundsen believed that the whole success of the expedition depended on them.

The dogs became great friends with the humans on board. They were a distraction against boredom amongst the men in the four months on the sea – especially as many pups were born after they left Madeira (21 by the beginning of November!).

Amundsen had worked extensively with dogs and sledges. He also had two excellent sledge drivers on his team. All his men were brilliant skiers, too (one was a world cross-country champion) and all had been skiing since childhood. He knew that Scott and most of his team had little knowledge of how to use skis properly.

However, Amundsen knew – from all the publicity surrounding Scott's preparations – that the British had three motor sledges. Amundsen feared these new-fangled machines might beat his team of traditional dog sledges to the Pole. It was possible that Scott might win before Amundsen had properly started.

The *Fram* continued south. She didn't call ashore again between Madeira and the Bay of Whales in Antarctica because Amundsen didn't want anyone to have the opportunity to quiz him about his change of plan. The journey took four months and the time was used to start real preparations for the race. Now Amundsen's men knew of his true destination and aims, he could ask them to do tasks that otherwise might have seemed odd for an Arctic drift.

There were 19 men on board and Amundsen gave them all different jobs – for example, minor alterations were made to the sledges to improve their performance over ice. The skiing equipment was checked and double-checked. Other tasks included making paraffin tanks for the sledging journey – on his North-West Passage expedition Amundsen had noticed that in extreme cold paraffin seemed to leak from its container. He knew that if this happened on the sledging expedition to the South Pole it could leave him short of cooking and heating fuel, a life-and-death matter in the frozen wastes of Antarctica. New containers were to be made from galvanized iron with special seals.

By early December the men on the *Fram* saw their first icebergs. On 3 January 1911 they entered pack ice – but they were lucky: they were not surrounded and held back by it for weeks as the *Terra Nova* had been. Just three days later they were through the pack ice and into the open Ross Sea.

On 11 January they saw the Ross Ice Shelf and on 14 January they entered the Bay of Whales. The *Fram* easily made her way through the ice floes here, she was built for this. When they reached the solid ice they put out their ice anchors and on 15 January they began to unload – it was ten days after the British arrival at McMurdo Sound. Amundsen used sledges pulled by teams of eight dogs. At the same time work began on their winter base hut. By 28 January, the hut was ready for the men to live in. It was at 78° 50' South, about 690 miles from the Pole.

On 4 February, just after midnight, the *Fram*'s watchman heard strange noises and rushed up on deck, thinking that the ice shelf might be breaking up and falling into the sea. It was almost a relief when he saw a ship, the *Terra Nova*, putting out ice anchors. He rushed to get an English grammar book and a gun in case of attack, and then watched with suspicion as crewmen disembarked from the English ship and approached across the ice. He was amazed as he was greeted in a friendly manner – in Norwegian!

It was Campbell, acting-captain of the *Terra Nova*, who had spoken to him. Campbell had been just as surprised to see the *Fram*. Campbell and the British learned that Amundsen (who was currently at the hut) was expected back at the ship early in the morning. They decided to wait to meet him. At six o'clock Amundsen appeared, driving his dog-sledge team swiftly over the ice to the ships.

The British crew showed Amundsen and his men around the *Terra Nova*, and told tales of how one of the mess tables had lain directly under where the ponies had been stabled on the ship. Consequently, on the voyage from New Zealand, urine and other horrible things used to drip through on to the table – particularly disgusting during a meal! One of the Norwegians said afterwards, "*I must confess it did not look very inviting!*"

But the British did impress the Norwegians with their food. The Norwegians had brought only plain and basic food to Antarctica with them but the British had luxuries such as tinned pheasant! As they all lunched together on the *Terra Nova* it seemed like a banquet to Amundsen and his men. Both groups of men spent the meal in good spirits but tried hard to find out each other's plans for the Pole. Neither gave anything away. No mention was made of the motor sledges. Eventually Amundsen couldn't contain himself any longer – he asked if they were working.

Campbell replied that one was already on firm ground – he conveniently forgot to mention that this particular piece of land was the seabed! He hoped Amundsen would get the wrong impression, and Amundsen did.

When the two teams said their goodbyes half an hour later, the atmosphere was friendly but wary; each side thinking the other might have the advantage in the race to the Pole…

Scott

Laying Depots

January – February 1911

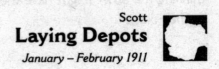

IF THE NORWEGIANS came away with a good impression of British expedition food, then the British were equally impressed by the speed of Amundsen's dog sledges.

Campbell and his crew had watched in amazement as Amundsen's men raced their teams of dogs across the ice towards the ships. They had never seen dogs pulling sledges that swiftly – or willingly – and they knew their ponies weren't able to go nearly as fast.

The British were also impressed by the *Fram:* by the space on board (everyone had his own cabin) and by the one central common room (the *Terra Nova* had two "messes" – one for officers and scientists and one for the rest of the crew). The *Terra Nova* had been far more cramped on the journey to Antarctica as there were many more men on board. Amundsen's expedition team was tiny compared to Scott's.

But both Scott and Amundsen followed very similar plans once they reached Antarctica. After unloading their ships and building their winter accommodation, each expedition aimed to start laying depots along the early part of the polar route before the winter set in. These depots were stores of food and fuel for the polar parties on their return so that they would not have to take rations with them for the entire journey to the Pole and back again.

From Cape Evans, Scott's only route across to the Ross Ice Shelf was over the solid sea ice. The land route over the back of Ross Island was blocked by terrible crevasses in glaciers coming down from Mount Erebus. The men knew from their earlier expeditions that this sea ice was likely to thaw as January progressed into February. It would then disappear for two months, so they would need to get going soon. It was only 23 January when they realized that the sea ice had begun to melt.

Scott knew that it was already too thin to take any huge loads so he hurriedly organized some men to take the ponies over the ice to Glacier Tongue. This was a long strip of ice, which seemed to be firmly and permanently attached to Ross Island. Meanwhile dogs, sledges and provisions for the depot journey were loaded back on to the ship, which was to sail to meet them at Glacier Tongue.

A day later, the sea ice they had crossed disappeared – the men and ponies had only just made it! After meeting the ship at Glacier Tongue, the team of 13 men, 8 ponies and all the 26 dogs made their way across the remaining sea ice on to the Ross Ice Shelf where they set up a camp. They chose a spot away from the edge of the shelf where ice was likely to break off. They called this "Safety Camp". It was from here that they moved their supplies out towards the Pole.

Their first depot-laying trip was to take them away from Safety Camp for five weeks. There were eight pony sledges and two dog sledges, together dragging a total weight of more than two tonnes. The ponies found the going very difficult. Their hooves cut through the surface of the ice, making them sink and stumble. As the ponies had been bought in Siberia they were used to snow and ice, but not to extreme conditions like this. Snowdrifts were a problem, the ponies often sank up to their chests and had to struggle out. Straining in the sub-zero temperatures of −15 °C and below, they worked up great sweats on their coats, which almost immediately turned to ice and made their work even more difficult and painful.

Incredibly, there was only one pair of snowshoes between the ponies, the others had been left at Cape Evans. Oates had no trust in this type of equipment, as he'd never seen it before, and felt the shoes would not really help. So Scott had agreed that they just bring one pair on this depot-laying journey to try them out. But when they were put on Gran's pony, Weary Willie, the pony floundered much less. Scott decided it would be better to travel at night, as the colder temperatures would give the ponies firmer ground to walk on and the warmer temperatures of the days to rest.

Each time the team started off, the men with the ponies would leave first. The dog teams would follow later because they travelled faster. This way it was hoped that both groups would arrive at the next point at roughly the same time.

The dogs performed well, pulling the three-and-a-half-metre wooden sledges of supplies over the ice and powdery snow with relative ease. Most of Scott's men now thought they were better than the ponies in these conditions, though Scott still wasn't convinced. He was not confident in their ability over rough terrain or with heavy loads over long distances. Nor did he trust them to remain obedient to their driver and keep going as they became tired and hungry over a long, difficult journey. On 4 February, he wrote: *"The dog lives for the day, the hour, even the moment. The human being can live and support discomfort for a future."*

The food allowance was 907 grams per day per man (unlike the 737 grams per day in 1902–1903). This seemed to be enough for the time being, when the supplies were being carried by the animals. But the dogs were already becoming thin on their ration of 454 grams of dog biscuits a day.

On 4 February the depot team reached a spot they called "Corner Camp", from where they turned due south. But suddenly a bad blizzard hit them. For those men who had never been in the Antarctic before it was a very new and frightening experience. As Cherry-Garrard, one first-time polar explorer in the group, said:

> *Outside there is raging chaos... Fight your way a few steps away from the tent and it will be gone. Lose your sense of direction and there is nothing to guide you back.*

Although very little fresh snow falls in Antarctica, blizzards are caused by the wind picking up the surface snow and ice, and whirling it around wildly. It is not only visually that things are chaotic: a thundering noise (like the sea in a terrible storm) sounds in explorers' ears, while the snow and wind gets in their ears and noses. They can find it hard to breathe and feel as though they are suffocating. Because it is so difficult to travel in a blizzard and so easy to get lost it is often better to sit it out in tents. This is what Scott ordered his team to do.

Cherry-Garrard noticed that during the blizzard the dogs dug comfortable holes in the snow. For the ponies, however, it was very different. Oates and the other men built walls of snow for them to stand behind to provide shelter from the worst of the blizzard. But in a swirling wind it was very difficult to gain adequate shelter without the cover of a snow hole or tent.

The ponies still had their summer coats. They had just travelled through the hot tropics in the *Terra Nova* on their way to Antarctica. They shivered miserably throughout the three-day storm, and by the end several were obviously thinner and all of them listless. Oates became very worried about them. In a letter to his mother he wrote, *"These poor ponies are having a perfectly wretched time."*

As the team marched on trying to set up the depots, some of the ponies became weaker and weaker. Though he loved them dearly, practical Oates proposed killing the frailest ponies so they could be left at the depots as food for the dogs on the following season's expedition (and even for the humans if necessary). Deep-frozen meat would keep in the ice almost indefinitely. Scott disagreed: he said it was inhumane to kill the animals. In his view, if they got weak they needed to be looked after like humans.

On 16 February the temperature fell to −21 °C. With a strong breeze blowing from the southwest, the men began to get the first signs of frostbite on their faces.

Frostbite is an extremely dangerous and unpleasant condition, which can result in loss of limbs, fingers, toes – and can even lead to death. To conserve heat in very cold weather, the body withdraws blood to its centre to keep the most important organs, such as the heart and lungs, warm. At first, someone with frostbite does not feel any pain as the area becomes numb. If the frostbitten part remains badly frozen it turns from white to dull-purple and will be difficult to move. This purple colour means the condition is very serious. If left untreated, the affected area will become black and either break away from the body, or become gangrenous and have to be amputated.

All Scott's men were now constantly looking out for the telltale white spots on each other's faces. Oates's nose and Scott's cheek showed whitened patches. These areas had to be rubbed and warmed quickly to prevent the frostbite developing. Lieutenant "Birdie" Bowers, who until now had travelled with just a green felt hat on his head (while the others had been in balaclavas and windproof hoods) had white ears. Bowers, who was nicknamed "Birdie" because of his big beak-like nose, seemed to be able to cope with much colder temperatures than anyone else on the expedition, but now even he had begun to suffer.

On 17 February, 24 days after the depot party had started out from Cape Evans, Scott realized it was impossible to struggle on any further (he'd wanted to go to 80° South). They'd nearly reached it, but not quite. Here at 79° 28' South, they set up their final depot and called it "One Ton Depot" (that was the quantity of supplies they put in it). It contained food for men on sledges, fuel for their stoves, pony oats and dog biscuits. A flag was stuck on the top to mark the depot's position. It was about 150 miles from Hut Point.

Scott had earlier sent the three weakest ponies back with some of the men. Now the rest of the group split up for their return journey to Hut Point. Scott went on ahead with Meares, Dr Wilson, Cherry-Garrard and the dogs. The other members came behind more slowly with the ponies.

On 21 February, Scott's group found themselves in a covered crevasse field. The crevasses themselves were hidden from view by lids of snow and ice. Wilson, who'd been on the *Discovery* expedition, wrote "*I knew from the noise and feel under foot that every now and then we were crossing lidded crevasses.*" Suddenly, to his right, he saw almost all Meares's dog team disappear – only the lead dog, the two final dogs and the sledge remained. The others dangled below over an open crevasse. Two had slipped out of their harnesses and had, luckily, fallen on to a snow ledge 18 metres below.

Meares was lowered down on a rope and, one by one, cut the dangling dogs from their traces and passed them up to the others. Only the two on the snow ledge remained.

Scott insisted on being let down himself to rescue them. While he was down there Cherry-Garrard heard him wondering aloud why this glacier was running at a different angle to the others in this area. Always scientifically alert, Scott wanted to be lowered to explore further – but thankfully the others dissuaded him.

When Scott returned to Safety Camp on 22 February he received a letter from Lieutenant Campbell. Campbell had decided to be left by the *Terra Nova* on Cape Adare for the winter and he would begin his expedition of the following year from there. The letter also contained the unsettling news of the *Terra Nova*'s meeting with the *Fram*, and the information that Amundsen was camped in the Bay of Whales.

Scott was horrified. This meant that Amundsen was already 60 miles nearer the Pole than he was! And, not only that, but he also had brought expert dog teams with him. Scott secretly feared these might be better able to reach the Pole than the ponies and motor sledges if they were well driven.

In his diary Scott noted:

> *There is no doubt that Amundsen's plan is a very serious menace to ours ... He can start his journey early in the season – an impossible condition with ponies ... the proper, as well as the wiser, course for us is to proceed exactly as though this had not happened. To go forward and do our best for the honour of the country without fear or panic.*

From his journal, Scott appears to have been remarkably calm about this unexpected news. But other accounts of his reaction vary. Cherry-Garrard later said that Scott was furious and described how he had, the next morning, passed into a *"state of high excitement bordering on collapse."* Cherry-Garrard said he had never seen Scott so distressed.

But Amundsen did not have all the advantages. As Wilson pointed out to Scott, there was a risk that the ice shelf Amundsen was camped on could fall into the sea.

He said, *"It will be a fortunate thing for him if the whole hut doesn't float out into Ross Sea."*

Unlike Scott, Amundsen was trying a totally new route to the Pole. If he met mountains he might not be able to cross them. He might find an impassable crevasse field on his part of the Barrier. At least Scott knew that the first part of his route was passable, lying along a route he, and then Shackleton, had taken in earlier expeditions.

By the time the remainder of the depot party had returned to Safety Camp, Scott was pretending that no one was racing him to be first at the Pole. No one dared talk about it in his presence – but they did when he was not around.

One of them, Frank Debenham, wrote in his diary:

Amundsen's chances ... are rather better than ours ... if [Scott] will consult his senior men I think it can be done, but if he keeps them in the dark, as they were on this depot trip, things are likely to go wrong.

Despite the bad news of Amundsen's challenge, Scott's immediate aim was to organize a second depot run and place more supplies on the route south before winter set in. The dogs were now tired and weak, and so were not sent out again. A group with a pony set out from Hut Point and reached Corner Camp. But, by 26 February, it was decided to turn back as the weather worsened.

Already the solid sea ice between the edge of the Barrier and Hut Point was beginning to break up. Scott and his men could either risk going over the fragile ice or take a more difficult land route over steep, rocky slopes. Wilson and Meares went with the dogs to try the latter, but Lieutenant Bowers (who had never been to a polar region before) set off over the ice with two other men and four of the horses. Scott, Oates and Gran stayed behind to nurse an ill pony, Weary Willie.

Bowers and his team, camping overnight on the sea ice, awoke to a loud noise. The ice had broken open, splitting their camp in two – right underneath one of their ponies, Guts. He had completely disappeared into the icy black depths. On the other piece of ice were their stranded sledges, but luckily the floes were touching and Bowers, Cherry-Garrard and Crean managed to drag the sledges across. Around them the rest of the sea ice had also broken up into floes; pieces of ice floated everywhere.

The three men now tried to lead the three remaining horses across the ice floes to the shore. It was no easy task. They had to wait until the floes drifted close together, preferably touching, and then encourage the ponies to jump across with them. But sometimes the floes bumped away from each other, or split apart on impact.

Gradually, they neared the safety of the shore. But their hopes were dashed again as another terrible threat appeared. A number of killer whales, hunting for seals, surfaced. The stranded ponies and men had attracted their attention as they crossed from floe to floe. The whales were clearly waiting for them to fall into the water.

The team had been struggling for six hours when they found a gap of about ten metres of open water had opened up between them and the shore. The men might have managed to make a dash for safety by leaping across the drifting floes, but they could never have taken the ponies with them in this way. Bowers decided to send Crean on ahead to alert the others and find help.

As soon as Scott knew of his men's predicament he rushed down to the water's edge. He ordered the two other men to climb on to the ice shelf using their sledges as ladders to get up and across it. Having got the men to safety, Scott started to devise a plan to rescue the ponies but, before they could find a way to get nearer to the animals, the ice started moving again. They looked on helplessly as the frightened ponies huddled together on the floe as it drifted slowly out to sea.

The men camped for the night and kept watch to see if there was any further hope of rescuing the animals. The next morning it seemed there might be. The ponies' floe had become lodged on a point of the Barrier a little way to the west and they rushed off to try to save them. But, as the men tried to lead the first pony to safety, he failed to jump clearly over a relatively easy gap, freezing and stiff from his night on the floe. He landed in the sea. The men struggled to pull him out without success. Oates decided to kill him with a pickaxe before the whales arrived and subjected him to an even more horrible death.

The next pony did manage to jump to safety – but as the third one took off a school of whales suddenly surfaced, making the pony swerve in mid-flight. He, too, landed in the water. As the whales circled, the men struggled to haul the pony on to the ice. But the poor animal was exhausted. Bowers had to kill him with the pickaxe to prevent him being eaten alive by the whales. It was a traumatic experience for all of them, especially for Bowers – this had been the pony he had been leading on the depot journey, giving him three lumps of sugar out of his own ration everyday.

The saddened men, and the remaining pony, Nobby, made their way to Hut Point to wait for the ice to freeze over again so they could rejoin the others at Cape Evans for the winter. Scott was amazed to discover that Glacier Tongue had completely disappeared in a storm – it had been a firm part of Ross Island since his first trip to the Antarctic.

He began to worry that a similarly rough winter storm might affect the base camp at Cape Evans as it was on a low beach. He had other concerns, too – the poor condition of the dogs at the end of the depot journey meant that maybe they were not going to cope at all next year, and, worst of all, his pony numbers had dropped to ten out of the original 19.

It was to be several weeks before the sea ice froze over again, allowing Scott and his men to rejoin the other members of the expedition at Cape Evans. The wait must have been very distressing and frustrating for Scott.

Polar Preparations
February – September 1911

AMUNDSEN CALLED HIS BASE in the Bay of Whales *"Framheim"*, meaning home of the *Fram*. There was one large hut and 14 big army tents, some were used for stores and others as kennels for the dogs. Nine men were to spend the winter there.

On 10 February Amundsen's team set off to start laying depots, as Scott was doing 400 miles to the west. Amundsen took three men, three sledges and 18 dogs with him, as well as half a tonne of supplies for the depot – mostly dog pemmican.

One man on skis, the forerunner, set out ahead of the dog sledges – Amundsen had discovered in Greenland that this was the best way to get the dogs running enthusiastically. They were all amazed at how perfect the conditions were for skiing and they covered 15 miles that very first day.

On 11 February, Amundsen wrote:

The dogs pulled magnificently and the going on the Barrier is ideal. Cannot understand what the English men mean when they say the dogs can not be used here.

With Scott's plan clearly on his mind, on 13 February he wrote:

Today we have had a lot of loose snow ... for us on skis it was the most magnificent thing going. How men [on foot] and horses are going to get through these conditions I cannot understand.

It was −12 °C. The Norwegian team were wearing their reindeer-skin ski clothes – which made them far too warm. Amundsen even ended up stripped down to his undershirt when driving the dogs! There was only one problem – some ski boots were too tight-fitting and two of the men quickly got bad blisters.

On 14 February they reached 80° South and built their first depot, filling it with the supplies they had brought with them. They had marked their way there with black flags on bamboo poles every eight miles. They came to the conclusion that these were too far apart and on their way back placed other markers in the snow every half-mile. Attached to every other marker was a piece of dried fish – they knew the dogs would find most of these, even if they were heavily covered by winter blizzards.

It only took the Norwegians two days to get home, covering 50 miles in the second day. The whole journey had taken only a week and the average speed had been 20 miles per day.

When Amundsen's team returned to *Framheim*, the *Fram* had already left to spend the winter in South America carrying out ocean surveys.

Amundsen wanted to do a second depot run before the winter started. He wanted to reach 83° South. Less than a week later he set out again taking all the men with him this time, except the cook, Lindstrøm (who said he was looking forward to having everyone out of the way so he could sort out the hut). During the interval Amundsen's men had unstitched and remade their skin ski boots, making them more roomy and comfortable.

On 22 February the eight men set off with seven sledges, each with six dogs. Once again, one man went out in front on skis. Conditions had changed – the temperature had dropped by 9 degrees and sledges and skis slid less easily. Then they ran into a blizzard. Even so, the team still managed 39 miles that day.

By following their old track, using the markers they had laid down previously, they reached 80° South after five days. Here they decided to remark the depot they had laid originally. They set out a line of black flags running east and west from it – ten on each side at half-mile intervals, all numbered and giving the distance of the depot from each flag. Even in really bad weather it was thought that the men would come across at least one of these flags to guide them to the depot.

The temperature now dropped to −35 °C, but still Amundsen's men were covered with sweat from the hard work of skiing. They had to sit up late at night drying their reindeer clothes over the stove in their tent but, incredibly, none of them ever mentioned anything in their diaries about feeling the cold.

On 3 March they reached 81° South and set up another half-tonne depot. At this point, with many of the supplies unloaded from the sledges, Amundsen arranged for half the men to return. It was now very cold, −45 °C: the going began to get extremely tough.

At 82° South they set up a further half-tonne depot. They were now within 480 miles of the Pole. The dogs were worn out and didn't want to continue (their feet had softened on the long boat journey – running on snow and ice would normally keep their paws tightened) and so the men turned for home.

On the whole it had been a successful preparation trip, despite a few disagreements. They had lost some dogs, but still had 85 left altogether (and 22 puppies). On the journey Amundsen had fed his dogs on dried fish and pemmican rather than biscuit, but even so they had lost a lot of weight.

The trip had given Amundsen a few ideas on how to improve things for the polar journey itself. For example, he decided they ought to have larger tents rather than two-man ones. So over the winter months Amundsen ordered that all the original tents were to be sewn together to make bigger ones. They ended up with dome-shaped tents that allowed the the wind to flow around them – much like igloos.

From 21 April, in the permanent dark of the polar winter, Amundsen set up a daily routine. The men woke at 07.30, worked from 09.00–11.55, then, after lunch, from 14.00–17.15, six days a week. During this time, the men made alterations and improvements to their equipment and prepared supplies for the trek to the Pole. In addition, each man looked after a team of 14 or 15 dogs.

By now a system of tunnels and storerooms had been built in the snow around their hut. Part of this network allowed the dogs to come down a tunnel to eat the toilet waste – a husky habit that saved the party the horrible job of clearing out the latrines.

Unlike Scott's team they carried out very little scientific work. But this wasn't the aim of their expedition, Amundsen's key purpose was to get the Pole. During the course of these intense preparations Amundsen had become more and more concerned about Scott and his motor sledges. He wanted to leave at the earliest possible moment when winter ended so he had the best opportunity of reaching the Pole before Scott.

Amundsen originally planned to leave on 1 November, but now he changed his mind. The departure date would be 24 August – the day the sun returned to Antarctica. Other members of his group thought this was very foolhardy, as it would still be extremely cold. But Amundsen persuaded them that they had to leave as early as possible. Reluctantly they agreed.

On 24 August Amundsen and his men were ready to leave with their sledges all packed (in fact they had been packed and ready for a month). But even Amundsen agreed that it was still far too cold (below −40 °C). Eventually, when the temperature rose to −37 °C on 8 September 1911, they set off.

But seven days later they were back at *Framheim*. The temperature had quickly dropped again to −53 °C. Their fur clothes had kept them warm during the day, but at night it was horrendously cold in the tents. Amundsen was persuaded to continue just to the depot at 80° South, dump the loads and then turn back. The retreat turned into a frantic dash for the safety of *Framheim*.

Amundsen rushed ahead with Wisting and Hanssen and arrived well ahead of any others. The rest of the group was separated and the final stragglers, with little food and no fuel, found themselves in a very precarious situation. In the extreme cold it was unlikely they could have survived another night. Fortunately they all made it back with nothing worse than frostbitten feet.

A furious row resulted between Amundsen and Johansen − Johansen accused him of failing in his leadership by rushing back ahead of the others, thus endangering the party.

It was now 19 September. Amundsen wondered how Scott was faring.

Scott
Winter and Spring
March – November 1911

SCOTT'S WINTER BASE hut at Cape Evans was run like a navy ship. It was divided into two (by putting packing cases down the middle). The officers and scientists were on one side; on the other the naval crew men, the groom and the dog-driver. (This divisional arrangement has often been used to criticize Scott, but it was typical of the time and especially of the navy.) Pride of place was given to the fully equipped darkroom and dwelling place of Herbert Ponting, Scott's experienced photographer, whose black-and-white photographs of Antarctic scenery have seldom been rivalled.

The inside of the hut was lit by gas and there was a stove and cooking range. In front of the hut, on the seaward side, there was a long, narrow building in which all the toilets were situated – there being separate ones for officers and men.

There was also a stable containing a blubber stove where Oates cooked up bran mashes for the ponies. Oates and the Russian groom, Anton Omelchenko, were in overall charge of the ponies. But each member of the polar sledging party – the Southern Expedition – was allocated a pony to care for and exercise.

Like Amundsen, Scott ensured that a great deal of preparation work for the Southern Expedition was completed over the winter. Equipment was made ready and repaired where necessary, especially the climbing equipment they would need to tackle the Beardmore Glacier. The motor sledges were oiled and tested.

One of the main tasks was to make a more nourishing food for the sledge-pulling dogs. About 400 kilograms of dog pemmican was mixed with seal meat to give them extra protein. Meanwhile Bowers reorganized the provisions for the men. Lumps of brown, precooked pemmican were taken out of their cans and put into cloth bags. Each bag contained a week's worth of food for four. (Later, though, the men would find it difficult to tell how much of the fat and meat mixture was equal to one meal.)

A great deal of scientific work was carried out by the British expedition team during the winter of 1911. There were several scientists, all with specific tasks to complete. Scott had a particular interest in these experiments. Scientist George Simpson wrote of him with high praise:

One thing which never fails to excite my wonder is Captain Scott's versatile mind ... He is constantly stating new problems and he seldom comes in from a walk without having made some useful observations. I must say he often sees things which have a bearing on my work which I have passed over without noticing their import.

On 27 June, in the midst of the Antarctic winter, Scott reluctantly allowed Dr Wilson to set off on a scientific expedition with Cherry-Garrard and Bowers across Ross Island to Cape Crozier. Wilson wanted to find the eggs of the enormous one-metre-high emperor penguin to take back to Britain. Scott asked the expedition also to test rations and equipment for the Southern Expedition.

The three men had a horrendous time. Cherry-Garrard later wrote a book about it called *The Worst Journey in the World*. They were away for five weeks in temperatures that fell as low as –60 °C. Man-hauling their sledges, they sometimes managed only a mile a day. Their wool and cloth clothing froze solid with their sweat, so they couldn't move their bodies properly. At nights they were horribly uncomfortable as their sleeping bags and liners were soaked by their own perspiration and then never dried out properly. But the men did manage to bring back three emperor penguin eggs. Cherry-Garrard later wrote, "*I do not believe anyone on earth has a worse life than an emperor penguin.*"

During the winter months, activities were arranged to keep the men occupied, including moonlight football and lectures on everything from "Horse-Management" (Oates) to "Scurvy" (Dr Atkinson). The men also put together a newspaper, the *South Polar Times*, in which Cherry-Garrard wrote:

> Probably anyone arriving here from England would be surprised to find how much work there is to be done during a long and dark winter. There are ten ponies to be exercised every day and they seem to get fresher every time they go out, and seals have to be killed and skinned. There is constant work on the sea-ice, collecting fish and other animals for scientific work, taking soundings and measuring the tides. With the care of dogs and ponies, meteorological observations, night watch for Aurora, working up the results of last season's sledging and preparation for the coming season, there is not much spare time … And so we live very comfortable … and we are all as fit as we can be.

(The aurora are naturally formed lights which move across the sky, especially occurring in the polar regions. The South Pole aurora is also know as the "southern lights".)

On 9 September Scott sent his first team out after the long winter wait – three men under his Second-in-Command,

Lieutenant Evans. Man-hauling a sledge, they left to check the depots. It was fortunate that they did so as some of them had been covered up by the blizzards and were difficult to find. Evans and his men cleared them and made them easier to locate.

It has been suggested that Scott's reason for sending Lieutenant Evans on this excursion was to ensure he was out of the way when he put his final plans to the rest of the men: Evans, as Second-in-Command, was probably the only man who would have dared criticize Scott.

In his absence, on 13 September, Scott announced his plans for his journey to the Pole. He had spent most of the winter agonizing over them, changing and re-changing the details. He had given the men a preliminary outline in May, but now he elaborated further.

Scott wanted to leave for the Pole on 3 November, admittedly a late departure, but he did not think the conditions would be good enough for the ponies until then. He had already seen how badly they had fared in the blizzards of the depot-laying journey. Scott calculated it would take 144 days to complete the 1,530 miles to the Pole and back. His projected return date was 27 March. He did not expect the temperatures to have dropped too low for human travel on the Barrier by then.

Scott described how they would use all four types of transport – motor sledges, ponies, dogs and man-hauling. The support parties for the polar team would lay depots as far south as possible. He wanted to rely on the motor sledges and the ponies – which could pull heavier loads than the dogs – to take the supplies across the Barrier to the Beardmore Glacier. The motor sledges would set out with fuel and food for the ponies; the ponies would pull light loads to Corner Camp and then heavier loads to One Ton Depot and beyond. The dog teams would pull more food for the ponies. Scott still felt that the ponies were far more reliable than the dogs.

Once at the foot of the Beardmore Glacier the motor sledges and ponies would turn back (if the ponies were terminally exhausted they were to be shot). Scott did not think that any of the animals would be able to climb the glacier. It was 1,000 miles from there to the Pole and back to Cape Evans.

The 12 remaining men would man-haul the sledges (four to each sledge) up the glacier, and continue to set out supply depots as far south as possible. They would use these depots to obtain fuel and food supplies on their way back so they could travel with relatively light loads on the return leg. Four of these men would continue with him to the Pole itself.

Scott's plans were obviously influenced by Shackleton's earlier success, getting to within 100 miles of the Pole with ponies and men in much the same way.

Bowers, spurred on by Scott's enthusiasm, felt that man-hauling was a very heroic way to journey on to the Pole – men working totally on their own without help from animals or machines. Bowers wrote in his diary, "*I for one am delighted with the decision.*"

Some of the Scott's men were less enthusiastic and didn't approve of the plans. They believed that it would only work in the best-possible weather conditions, especially as the amount of food supplies had been worked out for the exact number of estimated days' travel with little to spare. The scientist George Simpson wrote in his diary, "... *there is little margin, and a few accidents or a spell of bad weather would not only bring failure but also very likely disaster*." But they kept quiet because Scott was their leader and they were afraid of him and his temper.

With no public criticism from his men Scott felt able to write in his diary, "*The scheme seems to have earned full confidence: it remains to play the game out.*"

Yet, despite his own outward confidence, Scott himself was nursing concerns. He admitted in a letter to his wife that he was no longer confident of beating Amundsen to the Pole:

I don't know what to think of Amundsen's chances. If he gets to the Pole it must be before we do, as he is bound to travel fast with dogs, and pretty certain to start early. On this account I decided at a very early date to act exactly as I should have done had he not existed. Any attempt to race must have wrecked my plan, besides which it doesn't appear the sort of thing one is out for ...You can rely on my not saying or doing anything foolish, only I'm afraid you must be prepared for finding our venture much belittled. After all it is the work that counts, not the applause that follows.

On 15 September Scott took three other men, Bowers, Dr Simpson and Seaman Evans, man-hauling to the Western Mountains. Scott called it a "jaunt" to look at a glacier. But back at the base Debenham wrote, *"It was not quite clear why they were going or what they were going to do."* Long after his death, Scott was to be criticized for wasting his own, and his men's time and energy with this trip.

On 24 October Scott's men began to leave Cape Evans to set off for the Pole. Under the command of Lieutenant Evans, the two motor sledges took the lead, allowing them time to halt for repairs if necessary. The others with him were Day (the mechanic), Lashley and Hooper. Lieutenant Evans's job was, in theory, an important one, but it would also get him out of Scott's way during the final preparations.

During the course of the expedition Scott had come to the conclusion that Evans's skills lay in naval activities, rather than land-based ones. In a letter to his New Zealand agent, Scott wrote that Evans was:

> *...a thoroughly well-meaning little man ... but rather a duffer in anything but his own particular work ... not at all fitted to be "Second-in-Command", as I was foolish enough to name him. I am going to take some steps concerning this, as it would not do to leave him in charge here in case I am late returning.*

Scott decided to take Lieutenant Evans with the Southern Party as far as possible – he certainly didn't want him in charge of everything at the base camp for any length of time.

On 1 November Scott left Cape Evans with the pony party and made his way over the sea ice to Hut Point. Here the team discovered that they had left behind the Union Jack flag given to Scott by Queen Alexandra, the Queen Mother, for the special purpose of being placed at the Pole. However, he was able to telephone Cape Evans from Hut Point, ordering it to be sent on. (In September, Scott had arranged for a telephone line, the first in Antarctica, to be set up between the two locations). The best skier, Gran, delivered the flag into Scott's hands in three hours. *"The irony of fate,"* said Scott with a smile as he took it from Gran. A comment on the fact that the British flag had been carried the first few miles to the Pole by a Norwegian!

The Antarctic summer had arrived, and the sun was now permanently above the horizon. For the first few days the weather was relatively warm.

On 2 November the Southern Party moved on from Hut Point. As on the depot journey, they moved at night to give the ponies a firmer surface to walk on. The party set out in staggered groups at specific times. The first team was headed by Atkinson, with Wright and Keohane leading sledges pulled by the three weakest ponies. Two hours later Scott, Wilson and Cherry-Garrard followed with their ponies. Later Oates,

Bowers, Seamen Evans and Crean set off with the swiftest animals. (Oates's pony was Christopher, a wild animal that only he could control.) Scott had ordered Meares and the dog team to leave several days later from Cape Evans as they were much faster than the others.

On 6 November, just past Corner Camp, Scott was shocked to come across the abandoned motor sledges. A note left by Lieutenant Evans in the cairn at Corner Camp told how the motors had spluttered and periodically broken down before they had finally died for good – the second at 51 miles from Cape Evans. Evans and his men had spent hours trying to revive this one with no success. The note also stated that Evans and his men had carried on, man-hauling the supplies (as Scott had instructed in the event of the motor sledges breaking down).

Scott was greatly disappointed. He had been relying heavily on the motor sledges to pull supplies to the Transantarctic Mountains. They had proved they could take heavy loads but now they lay idle – broken and useless.

It was a bad day all round for Scott's team: the wind picked up and for two days all the men had to stay in their tents while the ponies huddled together behind the snow walls the men had built for them. Scott wrote:

> *It is not easy to understand at first why the blizzard should have such a withering effect on the poor beasts. I think it is mainly due to the exceeding fineness of the*

snow particles, which, like finely divided powder,
penetrate the hair of the coat and lodge in the inner
warmths. Here it melts, and as water carrie[s] off the
animal heat.

Scott had lost his motor sledges and now the ponies
looked likely to fail him.

Amundsen
Setting Off
20 October – 5 November 1911

AMUNDSEN'S TEAM FINALLY set off from *Framheim* on 20 October. This time he would take a much smaller group of five. After his row with Johansen, Amundsen had decided to leave him behind, even though Johansen was one of the most experienced polar specialists in his party. Amundsen's team was made up of Olav Bjaaland, Oscar Wisting, Sverre Hassel and Helmer Hanssen. All were good skiers and dog-drivers. The men took four sledges pulled by 13 dogs, each carrying 400 kilograms.

The depots were set up to cater for eight men and Amundsen had already allowed generous margins in his supplies. This meant there would now be an even bigger safety margin for his team with nearly twice as much food available as originally planned.

Their first target was the depot at 80° South. They encountered some very bad weather in the first few

The Norwegian Expedition's ship, Fram, *in the Bay of Whales, Antarctica.*

Roald Amundsen in his reindeer fur clothes and boots.

Captain Scott writing his journal in his quarters at the Cape Evans hut. On the wall behind him are photographs of his family including his wife and baby son. (7 October 1911)

Officer's quarters in the British hut at Cape Evans. Lieutenant Bowers (standing on chair) Captain Oates and Mr Meares had the top bunks, while Cherry-Garrard and Dr Atkinson were in the lower bunks. (8 October 1911)

British Expedition members getting the ill-fated motor sledge off the Terra Nova. *(8 January 1911)*

Captain Scott, Dr Simpson, Lieutenant Bowers and Seaman Evans man-hauling a sledge on an expedition to the Western Mountains. (15 September 1911)

Norwegian Expedition member, Oscar Wisting, and his husky team at the South Pole which they reached on 14 December 1911.

Polheim: Olav Bjaaland's photograph of Amundsen, Wisting, Hassel and Hanssen as they raised the Norwegian flag at the South Pole.

The five members of the British Antarctic Expedition who made it to the South Pole on 17 January 1912 (from left to right: Oates, Bowers, Scott, Wilson, and Evans).

We shall stick it out to the end but we are getting weaker of course and the end cannot be far.

It seems a pity but I do not think I can write more —

R. Scott

Last Entry

For Gods Sake look after our people

Last page of Scott's diary dated March 29, 1912. The diary was discovered eight months later with the bodies of Wilson, Bowers and Scott, together with undeveloped film of their final weeks at the South Pole.

days, including fog and howling gales. Even when the storm abated a strong head wind blew in their faces. Despite their well-marked route to the first depot they lost the way several times and at one stage found they had strayed into a crevasse field.

Wisting later remembered:

I came last ... with Roald Amundsen riding on my sledge. We sat back to back ... suddenly I felt a tremendous jerk in the sledge, which seemed to whip down by the stern, and wanted to glide backwards with nose in the air. I turned round quick as lightning and saw that we had driven over an enormous crevasse. Partly over, the snow bridge had broken under us, but on account of our high and even speed, the sledge luckily slid on to firm ice. We did not stop but continued on our way. Then I felt Amundsen tap me on the shoulder ... "Did you see that?" he said. "That would have liked both us, the sledge and the dogs." More was not said.

For the first few days the dogs were very excited and raced wildly. Some had to be bound on to the sledges to add more weight and keep the mad speed down a little! Four dogs that proved unfit were cut loose and left to find their own way back to *Framheim* (two did actually make it).

Amundsen and his team reached the first depot on 23 October. Despite the fact that there was a wild blizzard blowing, the five men and the remaining 48 dogs happily rested and ate the frozen seal meat that had been left there over the winter. The next day Amundsen wrote in his notes that they seemed to be *"enjoying life"*.

On the day they left the depot, 26 October, Bjaaland wrote in his diary:

Drove off 9 am. Dogs as if possessed, careered like madmen. Going good and terrain flat and fine. Distance 15.6 miles from 9 am to 1.30 pm.

Things were going well. Five days later, having spent one day trapped in the tent by a storm, the team had reached the next depot at 81° South. They had now travelled 140 miles. Their average speed had been three-and-a-half miles per hour. They covered the 15–20 miles each day in about five or six hours, which gave them plenty of time to eat and sleep. Bjaaland suggested they could do 25 miles per day, but Amundsen felt that they needed to keep the dogs (and themselves) fresh and not overwork them at this early stage of the journey.

After a few days' rest, Amundsen's team set off for the next depot. Yet again they found that they had strayed into a crevasse field. On one occasion, as Hanssen skied over a snowbridge behind his sledge, he slipped and fell. Knowing that if he tried to get to his feet the weight might cause the fragile bridge to collapse, he lay quite still.

His dog team, finding themselves temporarily alone and confused, had an enormous fight on the edge of the crevasse. This made the sledge to which they were attached move closer and closer to the chasm. It was on the point of toppling over the edge itself, when Amundsen managed to get there. Just in time he separated the fighting dogs, Wisting threw a rope to Hanssen and hauled him to safety.

On 5 November the team reached their depot safely at 82° South. For the last couple of days they had to navigate almost entirely by compass due to thick fog. Their main compass was strapped to a special sledge that had been made with no iron or steel that could upset its sensitive magnetic needles.

As they reached the depot the fog faded and the sun appeared. Amundsen and his men spent two days relaxing and resting their dogs. They dried out their fur clothes and discussed, as a group, their plans and ideas for the rest of the journey to the Pole. It was now only 480 miles away.

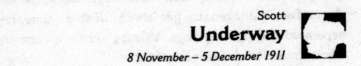

Scott
Underway
8 November – 5 December 1911

SCOTT HAD PRETENDED that he didn't care about Amundsen and had implied to his wife that he wasn't racing – but actually he was very worried by the Norwegian threat. He would have been horrified to know that the Norwegians were already over 100 miles ahead when he left McMurdo Sound.

On 8 November Scott's large contingent started to move off again, having spent two days sheltering in their tents from the blizzard. His party had now been joined by the two dog teams as well.

On 21 November Scott's pony and dog party caught up with Lieutenant Evans's team. The four men were extremely hungry and quite thin, after several weeks of man-hauling the supplies taken from the broken motor sledges. Evans had pushed them on and they had reached the appointed rendezvous location (at what was to become called Mount Hooper Depot) a week before Scott. While they waited there, they built a four-and-a-half-metre-high cairn, to keep themselves occupied. This was nicknamed "Master Hooper", after the youngest member of Evans's team.

From Mount Hooper Depot the entire group of 16 men travelled together – more or less. There were now five different starting times to cope with the different speeds of the various teams. The man-haulers first; then the three pony teams – each hitting a different speed according to the state of the ponies – and finally the dogs.

During this stage of the journey, their average travelling speed was between half a mile and two miles an hour – it was taking some of Scott's men more than eight hours to travel the 10–13 miles a day.

Not only were they travelling more slowly than Amundsen's team, they had far less time to eat, rest, sleep and recover each day than the Norwegians. Each night special snow shelters had to be built to protect the ponies, and these animals also had to be rubbed down and covered in blankets. All this used up the precious energy and time of men who had already put in a long day's work.

By now the stronger ponies were pulling loads of about 260 kilograms each, and the weaker ones, 180 kilograms. (The two dog teams pulled about 710 kilograms between them.) At One Ton Camp, Scott ordered a day's rest for the ponies and left a supply of seal meat at the depot.

Because the freezing conditions and the heavy pulling had begun to take its toll on the ponies, Scott decided to take the dogs further than he had intended. On 24 November the weakest pony, Jehu, was shot to give food to the dogs. Four days later Chinaman was killed. This time the men ate some of the pony meat. Much to their surprise they found it quite palatable. Bowers wrote, "*I must say that pony flesh is A-1.*" On 2 December Oates's pony, Christopher, suffered the same fate, as did Bowers and Cherry-Garrard's.

After 29 November Scott's men encountered a spell of better weather. At last, the endless monotony of the horizonless, grey-white skies and the southern-driven snow was broken. They could see the Transantarctic Mountains in the distance, which caused great excitement.

But once again, on 5 December, Scott's team woke to winds howling around the tents at 50 miles per hour. The snowflakes were bigger than anything they had seen before but the temperature was up to 1.5 °C! Bowers found it difficult to believe it was so high and he took his temperature recordings twice to make sure.

Forced to a temporary halt by the howling wind, Scott's men were trapped inside their tents, knowing that all the while Amundsen's team could be getting closer and closer to the Pole.

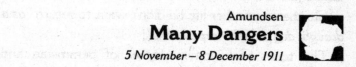

Amundsen
Many Dangers
5 November – 8 December 1911

During the two days of rest at his 82° South depot Amundsen discussed a change of plan with the others. Originally he had decided to go all the way to the Pole and back from this point without building any more depots. However, as they had found all the depots reasonably easily, Amundsen suggested that they continued laying more depots on their way to the Pole at regular intervals. By doing so they could significantly reduce the weight they were carrying on their sledges.

The men agreed that it seemed like a good idea. At that time, the dogs and the men on Amundsen's expedition were fit, healthy and well fed. But Amundsen and his men knew that this would be short-lived. Eventually the long, relentless journey would wear out the dogs, maybe even to the point of death. It made sense to lighten their load.

Hanssen later wrote of the scheme: "*It lightened the sledges for the poor dogs who would have to be driven and lashed forward if the journey was to end well.*" He also wrote that in another life he didn't want to return "*as a draught dog on polar expeditions*"!

The team took some supplies of pemmican and paraffin from the depot and set off again on 7 November. At two o'clock that day they passed the *Discovery* expedition's southernmost point of 82° 17' South and camped, as planned, at 82° 20' South for the night.

All the team were in high spirits. The fact that they didn't know what, if any, obstacles lay in their way didn't seem to disturb them. They all appeared to view the trip as a very long cross-country skiing and sledging race, rather than a dangerous journey of discovery across unknown terrain.

Amundsen's team was extremely well organized. Of the four sledges, the first was driven by Helmer Hanssen – the best of the dog-drivers. Just one word and a single gesture with the reins got the very best out of his huskies. Hanssen was also the best navigator and drove the special sledge with the protected compass on board.

Next came Hassel, another very experienced and able dog-driver. (Hassel had originally agreed to join Amundsen's expedition only until the ship got to San Francisco. However, Amundsen had always intended to take him as part of his polar team and had hoped that he would be persuaded to join him when he was made aware of the expedition's true aims. Luckily for Amundsen he agreed.)

Wisting drove the third sledge; he had learned dog-driving when he had been recruited by Amundsen. Driving the fourth sledge was Bjaaland: he wasn't as skilled at dog-driving as the others and sometimes found his husky team difficult to handle. At times he stated that he believed he had been given the worst dogs.

But Bjaaland was a top championship cross-country skier – the perfect man to have on this expedition when someone needed to go ahead to explore new, and potentially dangerous, territory. And this was just what Amundsen had in mind for the next stage of the journey.

Amundsen himself had no sledge, and so either went ahead as forerunner or travelled up and down the team as he was needed.

At this stage they were marking their route every third mile with cairns. Each cairn was made of nine large snow blocks, and was about the height of a man so it could be seen from the next in fair weather. Inside every one they placed a note listing its own position, its distance from the last cairn, and details of where the last depot was located.

Halfway between each new cairn Amundsen would stop to rest the dogs – there were 45 in the team now. He knew the huskies worked best with regular stops and he felt his men did, too. It was a good opportunity to make sure the whole team rested for a few minutes every hour or so. Routine was the essence of Amundsen's expedition and everything was aimed at the conservation of energy.

When they stopped for the night, the first thing the Norwegians did was unload the large tent. It was Amundsen's job to crawl inside, putting up the central pole whilst the others placed pegs around the outside, tying the ropes that held up the tent on to them. The dome-shaped tent slept five people and was made out of light, windproof material which had been dyed black so it would be easier to see in the polar landscape.

While the others finished off putting up the tent outside, untying the dogs and sorting them out for the night, Amundsen was responsible for getting the stove going and starting to cook the meal. It was easy to get the food from a sledge as it simply involved lifting up the lid of one of the provision boxes, which were permanently lashed on to the sledges. The men had spent the winter devising a system that would keep the boxes secure, but at the same time allow them to retrieve the items inside easily. Consequently the Norwegians didn't have to take all the boxes off the sledges every night to find what they needed – the normal sledging procedure of the time. This idea probably saved an extra half-hour each night and also each morning. When a meal was served, the sledge-driver from whose sledge the food had come noted it down in his logbook. This way an exact record was kept of what had been used and what was left.

When the dogs had been unhitched from their sledges and given their pound of pemmican, they were allowed to roam around loose until the next day. The Norwegians knew the animals would make snow-holes of their own to spend the night in. It was one of Bjaaland's jobs to take the ski bindings off the skis and bring in to the tent anything else that the dogs might chew on. Sledge dogs are a bit like goats – they will eat anything and everything! Finally a small, low wall of snow was built around the tent to stop the dogs peeing on it during the night.

Once the men and their dogs were fed, all they had to do was rest. Their sleeping bags consisted of three layers, starting with a bag of thin reindeer doeskin or calfskin on the inside. Then came a bag made of heavy male reindeer skin (weighing about 6 kilograms) and on the top was a cover of very thin canvas which absorbed the moisture from their breath at night. Ice formed on this layer rather than next to their bodies. Consequently the Norwegians had no problems with damp, wet bags making them cold and depriving them of sleep.

On 8 November Amundsen's team was still travelling over the Barrier. They knew that the Antarctic continent contained a plateau at high altitude. (Altitude is the height of something in relation to sea level.) Amundsen and his men were hoping against hope that the Pole might lie on the ice-shelf, not on the plateau – then they wouldn't need to climb any mountains or have any worries about the effect of altitude on their bodies. At high altitudes, in places like mountain peaks, the air becomes thinner making it harder to breathe and more difficult for the body to obtain oxygen. This can cause a condition called altitude sickness. The symptoms include: headaches, feeling sick, tiredness, weakness, dizziness, loss of appetite and difficulties in sleeping. At high altitudes the body gets dehydrated much more quickly and it is important to drink lots of water to keep the symptoms at bay.

On 9 November the team reached 83° South and here they built their next supply depot. By now they had got their building technique down to a fine art – from the surrounding packed snow they built up a cube two-metres square, placed the provisions inside it, covered it with snow and planted a black flag on top of it.

On 10 November, they rested for the day. The next night there was a bad storm, and when it was over Amundsen went back to see how their last cairn had been affected. Three of the dogs followed Amundsen as he went back: Karenius, The Sheep and Schwartz. When he turned round to call them they had vanished completely. (He concluded that they were trying to make their way back to find a female dog, Lussi, whom they had shot three days before.)

This meant that there were now only 42 dogs – and the three who had just gone astray had been Bjaaland's best. But Amundsen had always planned that, for whatever reason, the expedition might lose some dogs and so had taken along extra. The overall speed was not affected by the loss of these dogs as the expedition was not going at full stretch. Even so, Bjaaland was still finding it hard to keep up. But his spirits remained high. *"Sun and summer, splendid going,"* he wrote in his diary. He, like all the men, was clearly enjoying the journey.

Since passing 82° South Amundsen and his team had increased their speed to 20 miles per day. They were now covering one degree of latitude every three days. In all they spent six-and-a-half hours each day travelling and building cairns.

It was on 11 November that they saw mountains to the south of them – right in their path. They would have to cross them to get to their final goal. Amundsen decided to name the southern mountains the Queen Maud Range, after the Queen of Norway. His didn't know at the time, but these mountains form part of the Transantarctic Mountain range. Rising to over 3,600 metres the range runs 2,900 kilometres across the Antarctic continent.

Having read about Shackleton's earlier experiences, Amundsen knew that it was possible to climb mountains in Antarctica. But he also knew that Shackleton had spent two weeks trying to find a way up and he didn't have time for that – his team would have to begin to climb as soon as possible.

The Norwegians discussed the possibilities. The first thing they decided they must do was to place a depot at the base of the mountains. Here they would leave 30 days' worth of food and their sealskin clothing. It was proving too warm for them at that time, but would probably be necessary on the return journey along the Barrier when they might well be travelling after mid-summer. They decided to take 60 days' food with them. The reindeer-fur outfits and windproof outer clothes were going to go on with them, too.

On 17 November four of the group set off on skis to check out a possible route – eight miles to the south. Eventually they found a snowfield of fine and smooth snow, which they thought they could climb. The next day they tackled it. The going was very steep, but the dogs pulled amazingly well – over the steepest places the teams had to be doubled, but by that evening they had travelled ten miles and climbed 460 metres. They had also carried a tonne-and-a-half of supplies with them.

Their camp that night lay on a little glacier among huge crevasses, with towering mountain peaks on three sides of them. From here they could look out over the Barrier glistening in the midnight sun – *"the loveliest camp in the world,"* wrote Amundsen.

After supper three of the men skied off to check out the going for the following day – an excited Bjaaland returned saying that there seemed to be a path that could be navigated leading to a pass towards the summit! It was impossible to see if the plateau was beyond this summit, they just had to hope that this route did not lead them into another range of mountains.

The next day they climbed the pass – only to find a steep 250-metre drop at the top. It was only just possible to make it down the other side. They wound ropes round the runners of the sledges to help slow them down and to stop them sliding out of control. At the bottom of the slope they were faced with a climb across a small glacier. It was riddled with crevasses – but luckily these were well-bridged with packed snow.

After the crevasse field, they encountered another incredibly steep slope and all of the 42 dogs were harnessed together so that they could bring up two sledges at a time. The animals crawled on their stomachs, panting as they dragged their way up. Bjaaland went on in front so that the dogs had someone to follow. The men helped push the sledges from behind and called encouragement to the dogs.

Beyond this was another steep drop, even steeper than the previous one. Despite the ropes round the runners, this time there was nothing the team could do to stop dogs and sledges running into each other. In the commotion, Bjaaland's and Hassel's sledges were damaged.

Amundsen then turned his men a little westwards to head for a large mountain, probably over 3,600-metres high – it seemed that the route was pretty clear in that direction. But soon they found themselves above a great glacier – which Amundsen was later to name the Axel Heiberg Glacier. Often glaciers provide convenient pathways through mountains but this one was extremely steep and seemed to be pitted with thousands of crevasses – every step would be perilous. Amundsen decided he had to use it to move upwards: he didn't have the luxury of several weeks to look for another route. He had to keep moving on towards the Pole if he was going to beat Scott.

First they had to drop 600 metres to the glacier itself; then they started to move slowly and carefully over it. When they came to rest that night it was very difficult to find somewhere to camp. Eventually, when they did find a spot that was big enough to pitch their tent, they had to trample down the lumpy snow to flatten the ground. They had crossed nine miles that day and were at 1,220 metres above sea level – 490 metres higher than the night before.

The next day progress was slow but the weather favoured them. It was a dry, clear Antarctic summer day and Bjaaland led the way, climbing in his skis. His years of training for competitions was paying off here. The men set up camp at two o'clock, and Amundsen sent Bjaaland and Hanssen on to check out the route ahead. Eventually they saw a route, albeit hazardous, to the top of the glacier from where there seemed to be a path. It looked to be about 2,400-metres high. They hoped this was where the polar plateau began.

The next morning, 21 November 1911, they steeled themselves to set out again. It was a long, hard day – "*the hardest day we have had,*" wrote Bjaaland. But after 12 hours they were rewarded – they reached the top of the glacier. They could see no more mountains beyond it. The men and the dogs were exhausted. They went through the usual rituals of getting the camp ready, drank hot chocolate and ate a pemmican stew, before sinking, with great relief, into their sleeping bags.

Amundsen and his team had just travelled 44 miles in four days and climbed 3,000 metres with over a tonne of supplies through totally unexplored territory. The Norwegian had been both lucky and unlucky in his climb over the Transantarctic Mountains. Unknown to him, he had actually encountered the range at its narrowest point. Had he crossed only a few miles to either side it would have meant spending much more time in the mountains. But also, through ignorance, he had climbed the most difficult route in the area.

Amundsen knew that they could not have carried all the supplies so far without the dogs. On the evening of 21 November he recorded in his diary that the dogs had gone 17 miles with a 1,500 metres climb. *"Come and say that dogs can't be used here,"* he wrote. Nevertheless 24 of those heroic, hardworking dogs were shot dead before supper. Each man was ordered to shoot members of his own dog team whilst Amundsen, having no dogs of his own, prepared supper, trying to drown out the noise with the sounds of cooking.

Cruel as it seems, this had all been planned right from the start. Amundsen was only going to take the number of dogs he needed to the Pole. Only 18 huskies were needed for the final stage of the journey.

It was an evening of extremely mixed emotions for all the men. They had crossed the mountain range but they had been ordered to shoot many of the friends who had got them there. They consoled themselves with the thought that the dogs had seemed happy in the 18 months they had spent as part of the team. With grim irony the men called this place the "Butcher's Shop". It was 274 miles from the Pole. Amundsen wanted to rest there for two days after the exhausting climb up the mountains – in fact a storm was to trap the team for four days.

It was probably no bad thing to have that length of rest enforced upon them. It gave the men and dogs a chance to acclimatize to the thinner air of the high altitude. The surviving dogs had noticeably lost weight after the long climb – and were very hungry. Their dead companions were skinned and thrown to them. Amundsen believed, rightly, that fresh meat was needed to revive them. A diet of pemmican was not enough to keep the dogs going in these conditions. Amundsen persuaded his men to eat some of the dogs, too, and hunger soon overcame their horror.

C

By day five in the camp, 26 November, the weather was still very stormy but Amundsen was impatient and wanted to move on. He knew that every day he rested Scott was getting nearer to the Pole. Leaving one of the sledges at the Butcher's Shop, they continued their journey with three.

The visibility was terrible, at times they could hardly see the dogs in front of their sledges. Amundsen wrote, "*The going was … rotten – sticky as glue*." There were lots of drifts and it was heavy going for the men and the huskies. When the dogs started careering off down a very steep slope Amundsen ordered a halt. He couldn't see anything at all in front of him, so he had no idea if the slope ended in a sudden precipice. He decided to camp for the night and wait for the weather to clear enough to see again and work out the route. They had covered ten miles despite the weather. At three o'clock in the morning the storm cleared briefly. They got up and checked out the view: slightly to the east there seemed to be a more gentle snowfield that might take them down on to the polar plateau.

For the next ten days appalling weather led to terrible skiing and sledging conditions. The snow and ice was sticky and heavy, while fog surrounded them for much of the time. On 29 November they ended up on a glacier with horrendous crevasses and dangerous ice towers – towers that might have toppled at any moment, easily crushing a person below. They decided to call it Devil's Glacier. Crossing it took four days. Amundsen wrote the glacier:

> ... *proved to be worthy of its name. One has to move two miles to advance one. Chasm after chasm ... has to be circumvented ... the dogs struggle and the drivers not less. It is tiring for us two who go ahead.*

Once over the glacier, things did not get much easier for Amundsen's team. They now found themselves skiing in a complete whiteout over a sastrugi field. A sastrugus is a ridge caused by the wind on the snow surface. Sastrugi can be small – just like the ripples left in sand by the sea – but often they can be as high as several feet and look like the furrows in a ploughed field. Crossing them is like climbing over frozen waves and is an exhausting task, especially in a whiteout, when there is little warning of the next drop or rise.

Amundsen and Hassel, the forerunners, fell over sastrugi many times in the fog as they blindly led the way for the team. On 7 December, in a storm, they passed the 88° South point but they didn't lay their normal depot. Amundsen was determined to continue until he beat Shackleton's record of 88° 23' South – within 100 miles of the South Pole.

On 8 December they achieved it. The group cheered.

But Amundsen wasn't racing against Shackleton – this was a small victory compared to the one he now had in his sights…

Scott
The Beardmore Glacier

5 December 1911 – 9 January 1912

FOR FOUR DAYS, trapped by the storm, Scott and his men sat in their tents at the foot of the Beardmore Glacier waiting for the awful weather to subside. Scott wrote in his diary:

> *One cannot see the next tent, let alone the land...I doubt if any party could travel in such weather, certainly no-one could travel against it... It is more than our share of ill fortune .... how great may be the element of luck! No foresight, no procedure could have prepared us for this state of affairs ... it's real hard luck.*

Most of the men stayed in their sleeping bags in the tents. Oates, however, spent much of his time trying to comfort the frightened ponies. Evans described them, *"cowering behind their snow stalls, the picture of misery"*.

The men, the ponies and the dogs had to eat while they waited, using up precious rations. Scott had worked out the rations precisely for the whole journey, almost to the day. They simply didn't have enough food with them to spend days hanging around and by 7 December they had started eating into the supplies that had been put aside for climbing the glacier.

Finally, on 8 December, the wind began to drop. The men struggled out of their tents and pulled their sledges out from under snowdrifts that were over a metre high. Everything on them was soaking wet.

On 9 December the last ponies made their final trip, carrying their supplies to a point just two miles from the foot of the glacier. The snow left by the blizzard was now so deep that they were sinking in it up to their bellies. They were exhausted and starving, their food having run out a while before. It took them 11 hours to complete the last seven miles. Scott wrote in his diary:

> *At 8 pm the ponies were quite done, one and all. They came on painfully slowly a few hundred yards at a time... We camped and the ponies have been shot. Poor beasts! They have done wonderfully well considering the terrible circumstances under which they worked.*

The men buried the pony meat so the returning parties would have fresh food. Some called the place "Pony Camp", others "Shambles Camp".

The dogs fared better. On 11 December they were finally sent back to Cape Evans with Meares and Demetri Gerof. Cherry-Garrard remarked, "...*they have done splendidly. It looks as if Amundsen might have hit off the right thing.*'

Scott sent back a letter to his wife, Kathleen, with the dog team. He wrote, "*Things are not as rosy as they might be but we keep our spirits up and say the luck must turn.*"

That same day the men built a large depot, which they filled with provisions. They called this "Lower Glacier Depot".

Now Scott had 11 men left with him – each was expected to pull the equivalent of 90 kilograms of supplies up the Beardmore Glacier for 120 miles on to the polar plateau 3,000 metres above; quite an awesome task. Scott's sledge team consisted of Wilson, Oates and Seaman Evans; Lieutenant Evans had Lashley, Wright and Atkinson; Lieutenant Bowers led Cherry-Garrard, Crean and Keohane. The snow was deep and loose on the glacier after the blizzard. Scott was beginning to worry. He wrote in his diary, "*one has a horrid feeling that this is a really bad season.*"

With harnesses strapped to their backs and their feet in skis, the men pulled the three sledges. Bowers wrote that it was:

> ...*the most back breaking work I have ever come up against... The starting was worse than pulling as it required from 10 to 15 desperate jerks on the harness to*

> *move the sledge at all ... I have never pulled so hard, or so nearly crushed my inside into my backbone by the everlasting jerking with all my strength on the canvas band around my unfortunate tummy.*

The Beardmore Glacier is not as steep as the Axel Heiberg Glacier, but it is longer. It was a relentless, soul-destroying climb and it took them 11 days to reach the top. However this slow pace did give the British team some time to acclimatize to the increasing altitude.

Scott pushed his men forward until they were covering an average of 13 miles a day. But, pulling their heavy sledges behind them, it was taking them nine or ten hours. It was exhausting work. The men also had to keep a lookout for crevasses. Some of the men felt it was easier to see them with their goggles off, but this exposed them to the horrifying risk of snow-blindness.

As the team moved towards the top of the glacier, Scott worked out whom he would send back to base at Cape Evans next. It was a difficult decision to make, knowing that each man probably hoped to be in the final polar party. He chose to send back Atkinson (as leader), Wright (as navigator) with Cherry-Garrard and Keohane, both of whom he felt were weakening. This group turned round on 21 December.

The remaining men were split among the two sledges, which they pulled as teams. The first was made up of Scott, Wilson, Seaman Evans and Oates. The second of Lieutenant Evans, Bowers, Lashley and Crean.

Christmas Day 1911 was Lashley's 44th birthday. As he hauled himself up the glacier he suddenly found himself dangling from his harness in a crevasse. He was pulled out with much laughter as Cherry-Garrard wished him a happy birthday! Falling into crevasses was becoming an everyday occurrence for the men. Lashley wrote:

It was not of course a very nice sensation, especially on Christmas Day and being my birthday as well. While spinning around in space like I was it took me a few seconds to gather my thoughts ... It certainly was not a fairy's palace.

Then, on New Year's Eve, Scott gave a bizarre order, asking Lieutenant Evans's sledging team to leave their skis behind and continue on foot. His reasons for doing this are unclear. Perhaps it was another test, this time to see whether men pulled a sledge more effectively on skis or on foot. Or maybe Scott wanted to break Evans's spirit, making it easier to send him back. He knew Evans would be very disappointed if he wasn't selected for the final stage of the polar journey.

On 2 January 1912 they reached the plateau. Hauling the two sledges up the 3,000 metres over the last days had taken its toll on every man. But at least they had reached the top. They were only 150 miles from the Pole.

The next day Scott wrote in his diary, *"Last night I decided to re-organise."* He had decided to take four men to the Pole with him rather than three. It seems he had originally planned to take his own team of Wilson, Oates and Seaman Evans – Wilson because he was his closest companion and a scientist; Oates represented the army among the naval men; Seaman Evans perhaps represented the ranks – and Scott had enormous respect for the big Welshman who had been on the *Discovery* expedition with him.

But then Scott did something that went totally against all his preparations – he asked Lieutenant Evans if he could also take Bowers with him to the Pole. Everything Scott had planned so far – food, rations and equipment – depended on four men completing the final stage. But Scott's only comment after his announcement was, "*It ought to see us through.*"

Perhaps Scott thought he needed more manpower to pull the sledge – and that a fifth man would outweigh the disadvantages of taking an extra person. Or maybe he had suddenly realized that a second experienced navigator in the polar party would be useful.

Whatever Scott's reasons, it meant that Lieutenant Evans was now one man short to pull his sledge back to the expedition's base. But the decision had been made and the next day Evans's team nobly pulled their own sledge alongside the polar team for a while before stopping to cheer them on their way to the Pole, concealing their individual disappointment at not being selected.

Their return journey was terrible, with Lieutenant Evans very nearly dying from scurvy. His life was only saved by the great courage of Lashley and Crean. When they got to Corner Camp, Evans was left in the tent with Lashley while Crean set out on an 18-hour march to bring help from Hut Point.

The polar party suffered setbacks from the outset. Bowers did bring his own share of food with him, but within a day Scott was already regretting adding a fifth person to his team. He wrote:

> *...cooking for five takes a seriously longer time than cooking for four; perhaps half an hour on the whole day. It is an item I had not considered when re-organising.*

On 6 January Scott's diary describes how he and his team came across *"a sea of fish-hook waves"*. These sastrugi made it difficult to take a sledge across – certainly when pulling by skis. So Scott's men put their skis on the sledge and continued trudging on foot – they only managed 6.5 miles that day, much less than they had planned.

The next day, facing an endless horizon of sastrugi, Scott decided to ditch the team's skis thinking that this might reduce the weight of their load. He felt that there was no point in adding the extra weight to the sledge when they couldn't be used. But, after another mile, the sastrugi had disappeared and they decided to go back to get their skis. And they were very pleased they did. Scott wrote in his diary: "*I am awfully glad we have hung on to the ski* [at this time the plural of "ski" was "ski"]; *hard as the marching is, it is far less tiring on ski. Bowers has a heavy time on foot.*"

On the same day Scott also noted in his diary that Seaman Evans had a bad gash on his hand, which was taking time to heal. A few days before Scott had asked his men to shorten the sledges to lessen their weight now that there were fewer provisions to carry. Evans had cut his hand while working and it appeared to have become infected. "*I hope it won't give trouble,*" wrote Scott. Wilson also wrote about his concern for Seaman Evans. No one mentioned the word "scurvy" in their journals but all must have realized that a wound taking time to heal was one of the first signs of the disease.

The next day, 8 January, the men encountered their first blizzard on the plateau. It was not too severe but Scott ordered a day of rest, perhaps feeling the break might help Evans's hand. They were now at 3,200 metres – in the thin, exhausting, dehydrating air of high altitude.

During that day Scott wrote words of praise in his diary about all his companions. He gave Wilson a glowing report for being an excellent doctor, always on the lookout for the smallest ailment among the men. He talked of Bowers being meticulous and hard-working – a man who appeared not to feel the extreme cold. Seaman Evans was praised for endlessly maintaining the team's equipment. Finally, Scott commented on Oates's total commitment to the expedition. He concluded, "*Our five people are perhaps as happily selected as it is possible to imagine.*"

On 9 January they reached, and then beat, Shackleton's record. It was exactly three years to the day since Shackleton had been there himself. Scott wrote in his diary: "*RECORD.*" He just had one more rival to beat.

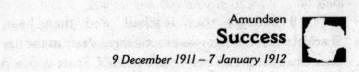

AMUNDSEN HAD BEATEN Shackleton's record exactly one month before Scott on 9 December 1911. He and his men stayed in bed a little longer the next day to celebrate. They built their final depot here, Wisting and Bjaaland taking 45 kilograms off their sledges. Hanssen, the ace dog-driver, was to carry on with the same amount as before. They marked the depot with great care. Black painted planks from empty packing cases were laid out leading away from the spot for about three miles – at 100 skiing paces apart.

They set off in good spirits, but their long, tough journey was beginning to tell on them. Amundsen, Hanssen and Wisting had frostbite on their faces and the dogs were becoming dangerous as they were extremely hungry. Amundsen wrote in his diary that at night the men had to regard the dogs as enemies, keeping watch for a possible attack at any time. One husky disappeared, probably leaving to die alone (as dogs often do) – they now had 17 left to drive the three sledges.

On 10 December they completed 16 miles as planned. All they had to do now was find the Pole. In a sea of flat, white land with no distinguishing features, Hanssen's navigation skills were put to the test. Using the special compass strapped to his sledge, Hanssen yelled directions to the forerunner. It was hard work for Hanssen, who had to drive the dogs, watch for bumps (which might overturn the sledge), and keep an eye on the compass.

On 14 December Amundsen camped at 89° 45' South, about 15 miles from the Pole. The next morning was clear and bright, and they packed up quicker than usual. The atmosphere was tense as Amundsen and his men began to look out for signs of the British team. Would they meet them on their way back from the Pole? Amundsen said: *"We advanced that day in the same mechanical way as before; not much was said but eyes were used all the more."*

"Stop!" called the sledge-drivers together at three o'clock in the afternoon to Amundsen who was in front. They had all been carefully watching their sledge compasses for the last few hours and they agreed they had finally reached the Pole! It was 15 December 1911.

They shook hands in silence. Then, as arranged by Amundsen the night before, all five men held the flag post together as the Norwegian flag was driven into the ground. As they did so Amundsen said, *"So we plant you dear flag on the South Pole and give the plain on which it lies the name King Haakon VII Plateau."* Amundsen and Bjaaland took photographs. (Bjaaland's were the only ones to come out. Amundsen later discovered that his camera was damaged.)

After the flag ceremony, one of the dogs was put down: Helga, the weakest of the pack, had only just made it – but Hanssen had insisted that his favourite had the honour of reaching the goal before being shot. The remaining 16 dogs immediately seized on the remains of their former companion.

The next day the Norwegians tried to take as accurate observations as possible to make sure they really were at the Pole. They knew they were definitely in the right area, but it was no simple task to calculate that they were at exactly 90° of latitude.

Amundsen set out to establish their position. He wanted to avoid any later suggestions that he had failed to reach the true Pole (as had happened to Peary and Cook after their North Pole expeditions). He knew his calculations had to be as exact and verifiable as possible.

It is easy today, in a satellite age, to fix one's position anywhere in the world using Global Positioning technology. For Amundsen it was vastly different. Compasses are not at all reliable near the magnetic poles. Accurate positions had to be fixed by making precise calculations based on sightings of the sun and the stars using a sextant (a navigational instrument long used by mariners). This required considerable skill and experience.

On 16 December, while Amundsen and Hanssen were using the sextant, Bjaaland, Hassel, and Wisting were sent to "box" their position, as Amundsen called it. Each man skied to a point ten miles from the camp, Bjaaland continuing along the original line of their course and the others at right angles to it, one to the right and one to the left. Each carried a spare sledge runner, three-and-a-half metres long, to which was attached a flag and a small bag containing details of the bearing and distance of the camp. When they had skied the distance, each was to plant the runner firmly, rather like a flag, and return. By "boxing the Pole", they could reasonably claim to have crossed the Pole at some stage, so long as it fell within the box (which it did). Moreover, it would be clear to Scott, who was likely to find at least one of these markers, that the Pole had already been reached by the Norwegians.

Amundsen calculated that their present camp was five-and-a-half miles from the true Pole and the next day, 17 December, they set out for it. Amundsen let Bjaaland lead the way as a mark of respect for the skiing skills that had helped him to win the race. When they estimated they had covered the distance to the true Pole they stopped again.

Amundsen and his men took navigational observations on the hour for a 24-hour period in teams of two (six hours at a time) and signed each other's navigational logbooks. Again, Amundsen didn't want anyone to criticize him in the way Cook and Peary had been for not obtaining countersignatures. Then the Norwegian team made souvenirs to take back home by scratching the date on to anything small they had with them, such as watches and knives.

That evening Bjaaland presented everyone with a cigar to celebrate. He himself didn't smoke, but he had carried them all the way from *Framheim* just for this moment!

The next day they set off to the place they had finally decided from their navigational observations to be the Pole – about one-and-a-half miles away. They were extremely accurate, this point was later confirmed as being just 200 metres from the true Pole – a fantastic achievement with old-fashioned instruments. The Norwegians had definitely achieved their goal. Nevertheless, Amundsen had the area "boxed" once more, just to make sure.

Several days of work in the area also proved to them Norwegians that no one else had ever been there before. There was no evidence of the British, or any other flag. Amundsen and his team were the first men ever to reach the South Pole and its surroundings.

They pitched their reserve tent at their final polar camp, which they called *Polheim*, "Home of the Pole". They tied the Norwegian flag to a long bamboo pole together with a flag from the *Fram* – the ship that had brought them from Norway to Antarctica. Amundsen left some equipment they no longer needed inside the tent. He also left a letter to the King of Norway inside a letter to Scott. All this would be evidence in case they didn't survive the journey home to tell their tale. He said to Hanssen, "*Scott will arrive during the next day or two. If I know the British, they won't give up once they've started.*"

"*Farewell dear Pole,*" Amundsen wrote in his diary as he left, "*I don't think we'll meet again.*" And so he and his men turned northwards towards *Framheim* and home.

◻

Amundsen was keen to be on his way and spread the news of his achievement. He very much believed that the first one to get the news to the outside world would get the glory. If news of the British team broke first, the Norwegian effort might all have been in vain.

They returned to their camp in the first polar "box" and picked up their tracks from there. The weather had been fine over the last few days and so the tracks were still very clear. This saved a lot of hard navigational work. Amundsen set up a flag at this point, judging it to be on the British team's route from the Beardmore Glacier. In the event that bad weather caused Scott to miss all the other flags in the area, Amundsen wanted to let his rival know that he had beaten him to the prize.

On the way homewards Amundsen and his team decided to travel by night so the sun would be behind them and they could avoid dazzle from the snow. They had 700 miles to travel to get back to *Framheim*. They travelled at a set speed of four-and-a-half miles per hour – covering a pre-planned 15 miles a day. It was a good speed in the thin air of high altitude.

Amundsen wouldn't let his team travel any further in a day. Consequently they spent 16 hours a day in their sleeping bags – resting and recovering. He wanted to keep his men as fit as possible for the return journey down the dangerous mountains. After that they would dash to *Framheim* as fast as they could.

At this stage, the dogs were weakening and gradually they began to die off. Three collapsed within days of leaving the Pole, including Amundsen's favourite, Lasse. Those who died were cut up and fed to the others. Of the original 52 who had started on the journey, only 13 were now left.

On 21 December, feeling more confident he was running to time, Amundsen decided to increase rations. It was clear that they were unlikely to run out of food before the first homeward depot. They reached this on Christmas Day. They now had eight days estimated journeying time to the next depot and food supplies for 12. The team was in high spirits. By 2 January they had reached the Devil's Glacier. The weather was better than on their first crossing and they were able to see an easier route through the crevasses and ice falls.

But despite Amundsen's meticulous plans, the team lost its way. For a while they had no idea where the next depot lay – and with it the beginning of the route down the mountain. They were debating whether it lay to the east or west of them, when a sudden, dense fog stopped all visibility completely and meant they could not go any further. They had to camp. When the fog lifted they made a decision to go westwards.

But there was no sign of the depot. After more debate, they agreed that the best thing they could do was to set off towards the Butcher's Shop and not waste time looking for the other depot. With luck they would be able to find the exact place where the dogs were buried. The men had enough food to get them down to the Barrier, but not the dogs – and none of the Norwegian team wanted to have to man-haul the sledges.

Suddenly one of the men recognized the lie of the land to the east and the team was able to work out the site of their missing depot. Bjaaland and Hanssen were sent with an empty sledge and the best dogs to retrieve their food. But it was a rougher and longer journey than they had anticipated – the Antarctic light had distorted the sense of distance. The pair soon began to worry about the fact that they hadn't brought any sleeping bags with them: they might not survive a night in the open.

Amundsen was very worried about the two men, and paced up and down, watching the weather, hoping it would get no worse. He was overjoyed to see them approaching on their return journey. It had been an exhausting run, but the pair had managed to reach the depot and get themselves back, ten hours later, with all the provisions.

Now the team had ten days' food for both men and dogs – plus emergency reserves. It should only take five days to reach the next depot. Even if things went wrong in the mountains they were well prepared. Amundsen was able to relax a little.

As the weather had improved Amundsen decided they should set off as soon as possible to the Butcher's Shop and then down the mountains. Having lost their way once in this area, he realized it was better to do as much travelling as possible when they could see where they were going. Consequently, on 4 January they covered 20 miles and, after five hours rest, continued on again. After a further ten miles they saw the line of cairns – they were back on track! The next day they reached the Butcher's Shop.

But the landscape seemed to have changed – six weeks earlier they had only been able to glimpse parts of it through thick fog. Now they realized how dangerous it had been to travel so blindly through the mountains. It was only with a great deal of skill and detective work that Hanssen was able to track down the depot containing the dog carcasses using his compass.

Before they set off down the Axel Heiberg Glacier, they fed the dogs with some of the meat and then put a carcass on each sledge for later. Amundsen and his men didn't want to hang around at the Butcher's Shop. The temperature had dropped to –25 °C, five degrees lower than they had been used to on the plateau. A freezing wind put a chill into their bones that they hadn't experienced on their trip to date. Were these the first signs of the approaching Antarctic winter?

They set off quickly, with Bjaaland leading the way. Once again they wrapped rope round the sledge runners and within half an hour had descended 900 metres. How different this part of the journey was to the way up, when the dogs had been crawling along on their stomachs, straining to haul the sledges behind them! The team camped at 2,300 metres.

At one o'clock in the morning they got up to set off again. The skiers, Amundsen, Bjaaland and Hassel, were clearly enjoying the challenge of the downhill run and were having fun. "*We whizzed down. A wonderful sport*," wrote Amundsen. Bjaaland wrote, "*The skiing was wonderful. I had many good runs and raced with the Captain.*"

But the dog-drivers were not enjoying the run so much. Even with ropes wound round the runners, driving a sledge down a very steep slope, trying to avoid ice falls and chasms, is not at all easy. The dogs were sinking up to their knees in the loose snow as they made their descent. But the animals had confidence in their drivers and kept going – they seemed to know they were on their way home. Eleven-and-a-half miles later, having dropped 1,400 metres, they decided to camp in the very same place they had camped 47 days before. So much had happened since then – and now they knew that the worst part of their journey was probably over.

The Norwegians realized that the Axel Heiberg Glacier made its way right down on to the Barrier close to their last Barrier depot. And so, on their final day in the mountains, they continued straight on down the glacier, turning north when they reached the great ice shelf.

Just before midnight on 7 January they arrived at their depot at 85° 5' South. Such was the speed of their progress they found they now had food for 35 days. It was far more than they needed for the journey back to *Framheim*. And they still had other depots set up in front of them on their route.

Scott
"A Terribly Trying Time"
10 January – 17 February 1912

SCOTT'S TEAM KEPT trudging towards the Pole; the weight of the sledge dragging heavily behind them. Bowers stumbled along on foot, often sinking into the snow, as he walked alongside the skiers. All around the tiny team of men was the vast whiteness of the polar plateau, there was no horizon, nothing to give any point of interest at all to the view. Scott wrote: *the marching is growing terribly monotonous.*

On 10 January they set up a cairn at 88° 29' South in which they left a week's supply of food and some surplus clothing. This lightened the load on the sledge by about 45 kilograms. They were now carrying about 18 days' supply of food and they reckoned they were about 97 miles from the Pole. Over the next few days Scott and Wilson recorded in their diaries how soft the snow was and how difficult it was to pull the sledge across it.

After the climb up the Beardmore Glacier, the men were already totally drained of energy. So now, at a high altitude, they had very few reserves of strength left to draw upon. To top it all, their food supply was limited and they had to be careful with their provisions: they were beginning to starve.

The daily food ration at this point was a mug of warm pemmican stew at breakfast and dinner, and a lunchtime biscuit. Each of these meals was accompanied by a cup of tea. This meant their liquid intake was very low, less than three litres per day. They were probably all now becoming very dehydrated – not only were they losing moisture through marching and pulling their sledge over difficult ground, but they were also working in a very dry environment.

On 11 January Scott wrote:

Another hard grind in the afternoon and five miles added. About 74 miles from the Pole – can we keep this up for seven days? It takes it out of us like anything. None of us ever had such hard work before ... our chance still holds if we put the work in, but it's a terribly trying time.

The team now started to feel the cold more and increasing amounts of hair fell out of their reindeer-fur boots. In his diary, Scott wrote that Oates seemed to be suffering from the intensity of the cold even more than the rest of them, and to be the most tired.

After the daily 12-hour trudge in difficult conditions, setting up camp at night was inevitably a lengthy chore. It took time to unlash the packing cases, take them off the sledge and remove the provisions from the boxes.

As they had seen no trace of the Amundsen expedition on the Beardmore Glacier they had discussed the possibility that he had met with an accident. All of them assumed that Amundsen would have used Shackleton's tried-and-tested route to take him most of the way to the Pole. It hadn't really occurred to them that he might have used a totally new and unexplored route all the way from his base camp. On 15 January they set up another depot and filled it with nine days' worth of provisions. In his diary, Scott wrote of: *"the only appalling possibility, the sight of the Norwegian flag forestalling ours … only 27 miles from the Pole."*

The next morning the team marched well, covering seven-and-a-half miles. They were not expecting to reach the Pole until the next day.

In his diary Scott states:

...we started off in high spirits in the afternoon, feeling that tomorrow would see us at our destination. About the second hour of the march Bowers's sharp eyes detected what he thought was a cairn; he was uneasy about it, but argued that it must be a sastrugus. Half an hour later he detected a black speck ahead. Soon we knew this could not be a natural snow feature. We marched on...

As they grew closer they realized a black flag was fluttering in their path. It was the flag that Amundsen had placed where he thought Scott's route to the Pole from the Beardmore Glacier would cross his own. Paw prints remained in the snow all around the spot. It was five o'clock on 16 January 1911 and any last spark of energy and hope drained from the explorers' bodies. They had lost the race. All their effort over the last long days, weeks and months had come to nothing.

Despite their tiredness, all the men found it difficult to sleep that night.

Scott recorded:

> *The worst has happened, or nearly the worst... The Norwegians have forestalled us and are first at the Pole. It is a terrible disappointment and I am very sorry for my loyal companions... All the daydreams must go; it will be a wearisome return.*

Bowers wrote:

> *...it is sad that we have been forestalled by the Norwegians, but I am glad that we have done it by good British man-haulage. That is the traditional British sledging method and this is the greatest journey done by man since we left our transport at the foot of the glacier.*

Oates wrote:

We are not a very happy party tonight... Scott is taking his defeat much better than I expected... Amundsen – I must say that that man must have his head screwed on right... The Norskis ... seem to have had a comfortable trip with their dog teams, very different to our wretched man-hauling.

Scott was devastated, but he decided they had to go on to the Pole themselves and raise the British flag there, even though he probably knew it was best to return to base camp as soon as possible as the food situation was so perilous.

On Wednesday 17 January at half past six in the evening, they dragged their sledge to what they considered to be the Pole. Scott wrote:

Great God! this is an awful place and terrible enough for us to have laboured to it without the reward of priority.

They took observations and, like Amundsen, decided the true Pole was probably really about three miles away.

The next morning they started out towards it at five o'clock. But what they saw was Amundsen's tent with the Norwegian flag flying on the top. Inside Scott found Amundsen's letter:

Dear Captain Scott

– as you are probably the first to reach this area after us, I will ask you kindly to forward this letter to King Haakon VII. If you can use any of the articles left in the tent, please do not hesitate to do so.

With kind regards. I wish you a safe return.

Yours truly

Roald Amundsen

Scott's men looked around and to their relief and amazement found the Norwegians' good fur clothing. Bowers was particularly grateful to get a pair of reindeer-fur gloves. He had been pulling the sledge for several days with no gloves at all since he had lost his dogskin ones.

The British left a note in the tent to say that they had been there, and set off to take photographs of themselves. They placed the Union Jack at a spot they believed to be within about half a mile of the Pole – about one-and-a-half miles away from Amundsen's *Polheim*. The photographs show a band of cold and tired men – there is no sense of jubilation at all in any of their faces.

They turned to go back. There were 800 miles before them – 800 miles to drag the sledge. They followed their own tracks and found their way back past the Norwegian flag they had first seen. As planned, they began to use the strong wind that had so hindered them on the way south to help push themselves northwards. They fixed a sail to the sledge – using the pole (an old sledge runner) from Amundsen's flag as the mast.

On the 17 January Scott wrote, "*Now for the run home and a desperate struggle to get the news through first. I wonder if we can do it.*" (The phrase "*to get the news through first*" was omitted from the original published version of Scott's journal.)

During the next three weeks Scott and his men travelled surprisingly far for men in their condition – an average of 14 miles a day. When they could, they erected the sail on the sledge and let the following wind carry them along. But even with their backs to the wind it seemed that they were feeling the cold much more than before. The average temperature had dropped to around –34 °C.

On several occasions they were trapped in their tents by blizzards. Scott was worried and wrote of the unsettled nature of the weather, "*Blizzards are our bugbear, not only stopping our marches, but the cold damp air takes it out of us.*" Their sleeping bags were getting damper and damper, and there was little hope of drying them out. As the "midsummer" point had passed, it could only get colder.

When the wind wasn't suitable for "sailing" the team had to trudge along pulling the heavy sledge behind them. Their ski boots were beginning to wear out. They reached their depots, ravenous for the food that was stored in them. They were probably eating only half the food they needed for the hard work of man-hauling. They were slowly starving.

There were growing problems with the health of the group. Evans's fingers were badly blistered with frostbite. He was usually a jolly man, but now seemed very gloomy and cross with himself. Oates was also getting frostbitten and he seemed almost constantly to have cold feet. In the photograph of the team at the Pole Oates is leaning heavily on one leg – it is likely he was feeling a lot of pain from an old war wound at this point and frostbite was probably beginning to set severely into his feet. Wilson strained a tendon in his leg, which meant he couldn't help pull the sledge for a few days. He also kept suffering from snow-blindness as he persisted in taking off his goggles to see better for sketching. Scott himself fell on a very slippery surface and hurt his shoulder quite badly.

Bowers was the only one who didn't seem to be suffering too much from the arduous journey. On 31 January he retrieved his skis, which he had abandoned on New Year's Eve. He had just plodded through 360 miles of snow without them – a remarkable achievement. He had written in his diary not long before, "*...soft plodding for me on foot. I shall be jolly glad to pick up my dear old ski.*"

On Sunday 4 February the struggling group suddenly found themselves in a crevasse field. Evans fell into two – the second time with Scott. These were minor accidents in normal mountaineering circumstances. However, Evans seemed to become more clumsy as a result. (It is possible that he had burst a blood vessel in his brain in one of the accidents.)

It was not until 7 February that the team began to make its way down the Beardmore Glacier. They were relieved to reach it. Scott recorded in his diary that if Evans had had to continue for another week at a high altitude it would have had a very serious effect on him. Scott also wrote that seeing rock in the mountains after the relentless snow and ice of the plateau was, *"like going ashore after a sea voyage."* But they all continued to worry about food. They had five days' worth of provisions as they started to descend down the glacier – and it was five days to the next depot. There was no time to spare.

Yet, incredibly, Scott agreed that Wilson could spend an afternoon collecting rock samples from the Transantarctic Mountains to take back for research. Scott ordered Evans and Oates to sit in the sun while the others searched with Wilson. Perhaps Scott felt that a rest in the warmer weather at a lower altitude would help prevent Evans from weakening further. But some modern commentators have criticized Scott for wasting precious time and adding more weight to the sledge.

For three days the men struggled with the sledge over a huge crevasse field. One or other of the group seemed to fall into a crevasse every few minutes. Fortunately, the ropes always held and they were hauled out again by their companions. But they knew that a huge chasm could open underneath them at any moment and swallow them all up for good.

It was then that the team lost their way. They had not set out any markers to their depot cairns on their way up, so there were no signs at all to help lead them to the next supply of food and fuel. A fog enveloped them and Scott became more and more worried that his team was going to miss the next depot. Having no food supplies in reserve on their sledge, they could ill afford to do that.

But luck smiled briefly on them. The fog cleared for a short while, and Wilson caught sight of the flag on the Mid-Glacier Depot. They pulled the sledge towards it with relief. It was now 13 February.

The strain of the journey was seriously beginning to tell on all the men. Now they had come off the high plateau they needed rest and good food – but neither was available. They had to keep going, as fast as their condition would allow, if they were to reach food and, ultimately, safety.

The next day Evans discovered a huge blister on his foot. He was slowing down and finding it difficult to put on his crampons to cross the crevasse field. On 12 February Oates wrote:

...it's an extraordinary thing about Evans, he's lost his guts, and behaves like an old woman or worse. He's quite worn out with the work, and how he's going to do the 400 odd miles we've still got to do, I don't know.

Scott recorded Saturday 17 February 1912 as a *"very terrible day"* in his diary. Evans had collapsed the day before, was sick and giddy and unable to continue. Even skiing beside the sledge was beyond him. Scott decided to camp there and then to give him some rest. The next morning Evans declared (as always) that he was quite well, and they all set off again on their skis, pulling the sledge.

But Evans hardly seemed to be aware of what was going on around him as he stumbled along. After about half an hour his ski boots came undone and he stayed behind to fix them while the others continued with the sledge. An hour or so later they stopped and waited while he slowly caught up with them. Together they all set off with the sledge but again, after 30 minutes or so, he dropped out for the same reason.

By lunchtime Evans hadn't caught up with the rest of the men so they went back on skis to help him. Scott reached him first and found him crawling in the snow, *"...on his knees with clothing disarranged, hands uncovered and frostbitten, and a wild look in his eyes."* He was suffering from a mixture of malnutrition, exhaustion, the effects of severe frostbite, probably scurvy and a possible slow brain haemorrhage.

Scott arranged for Oates to stay with him while he, Wilson and Bowers went back for the sledge. They emptied it of its supplies, and took him back to the tent on it. By now Evans had lost consciousness.

He died a little while later.

Towards *Framheim*

11 January – 7 March 1912

ONCE THEY HAD REACHED the bottom of the Transantarctic Mountains, Amundsen and his team began racing up across the Barrier towards *Framheim*.

They were now travelling for up to 20 miles before camping, resting for eight hours and then setting off again. They didn't worry if it was day or night, the sun was always there and it was always light. Their aim was to get back to *Framheim* as soon as possible so they could be the first to tell the world of their victory. Amundsen didn't want Scott to steal his thunder.

On 11 January the mountains disappeared from view behind them. They were now halfway between the Pole and *Framheim*. On the same day they saw two birds – skuas – the first wildlife they had seen for a very long time. Amundsen felt they were a sign that he and his team were approaching the world of the living again.

Bjaaland wrote in his diary:

> *Good day, good day, dear skua-crow. How are you*
> *doing? ....You go back to Lindstrøm and tell them we'll*
> *be there in 20 days and clean up his hot cakes, beef and*
> *fruit even if it's green plums.*

The weather was not good for the Norwegians – they had storms and fog, wild winds and much snow whirling around them, but they raced on regardless. Even in the worst weather, it was seldom a problem finding the depots. The cairns they had set up between the depots on their outward journey now proved their worth. At their faster pace the men only spent two, or at the most three, days between each depot. But they didn't really need the contents – they had more than enough food with them to complete the journey back to *Framheim*. The dogs and the humans were gorging themselves on seal meat, pemmican and lots of chocolate. They even started to put on weight!

On 17 January they were at depot 82° South – the last one they had set up before the previous winter. Amundsen wrote:

> *...we had a special meal to celebrate our arrival at*
> *civilization's furthermost outpost in the south. Wisting*
> *has to be cook on such occasions. He plied us with a*
> *mixture of pemmican and seal steak. For dessert:*
> *chocolate pudding.*

They now felt they were almost within sight of *Framheim*. There was a line of flags to follow for the last 200 miles. They skied on with great excitement even though the weather was, for the most part, bad. They were now covering up to 30 miles a day; nothing seemed to stop them or slow them down. Their spirits were high – they were well fed, they had won the race, and they were on their way home.

On 25 January Amundsen and his men were just 18 miles from *Framheim*. But then they lost their course in a bad fog – they couldn't even see the tips of their skis. When it cleared there was not a flag in sight. How could they be so near to home and yet so lost? They studied their compasses carefully and set off again. Eight miles later they spotted an object to their west. On closer examination it turned out to be a sledge that they had left behind on 20 October when they had first started out from base – just over four months before. They now knew their exact position.

On Friday 26 January they returned to the Bay of Whales and skied down to *Framheim*. They had travelled a vast 1,004 miles in only 99 days.

It was four o'clock in the morning. The four men at the base were asleep. Amundsen had deliberately arrived at that time to surprise them – the polar team wasn't expected back for another ten days.

Amundsen walked quietly into the hut.

"*Good morning, my dear Lindstrøm,*" he said, "*do you have any coffee for us?*"

The sleeping man woke with a shock. "*Good God, is it you?*" said Lindstrøm. Then he called out to the others, "*Get up, boys, it's the first cuckoo of spring.*"

They shook hands all round. Someone finally asked the big question and Wisting recorded the moment:

> *"Have you been there?" "Yes, we've been there,"* *answered Roald Amundsen, and then there was a* *hullabaloo. Soon after, we were all seated round the* *table and savoured Lindstrøm's hot cakes and heavenly* *coffee. How good a cup of coffee can really taste one only* *realizes when, like us, one has to go without so long.*

There was a short speech from Amundsen, who praised the four men in his polar team and said that they all worked well together and had had no quarrels. At the end of the meal schnapps, a special alcoholic drink, was handed out – they celebrated in style!

While they had been away, Prestrud, Johansen and Stubberud had journeyed out to King Edward VII Land and, on 29 November, became the first people to set foot there.

By coincidence, the day after Amundsen's return, the *Fram* arrived back in the Bay of Whales. When the captain, Milsen, saw the Norwegian naval ensign flying from Cape Man's Head (the prearranged signal to say that the polar party had returned safely) he hooted the siren again and again. The men rushed out to meet the ship amid great excitement.

Amundsen was keen to leave the Antarctic as soon as possible and to get his news back to the outside world. He still feared that, even if Scott hadn't beaten him to the Pole, he would beat him to the press. Amundsen and his team hurried to pack up. They took only the most valuable equipment with them, but it still took them two days, in relays, to ferry it all across the solid sea ice to the *Fram*.

Even in their haste they still gave themselves time to have a final "Farewell to *Framheim*" dinner on the Sunday, with Lindstrøm producing some champagne. (He had spent all winter sleeping with the bottles in his bed so they wouldn't get too cold and burst!)

The team had achieved everything they had set out to do including visiting King Edward VII Land, and carrying out the first oceanographic survey of the South Atlantic between America and Africa. But the biggest prize by far was the Pole.

On the evening of 30 January Amundsen firmly shut the door of *Framheim* for the last time. Lindstrøm had cleaned it from top to bottom before they left. It was *"shining like a new pin,"* said Amundsen, *"… we wouldn't be accused of untidiness or dirt if anyone should happen to go there and look."*

When they left they took the 39 remaining dogs with them. Amundsen wrote about the animals' reaction to being back on the *Fram* again:

Strange to see how many of the old veterans immediately recognized Fram's deck. Wisting's sturdy dog, Old Colonel, with his two adjutants, The Whopper and Arne, immediately took the place where they had stood many a fine day during the long voyage south ... Mylius and Ring – Helmer Hanssen's special favourites – began playing there in the corner of the fo'c'sle to port, as if nothing had happened. Nobody could see by the two jolly rascals that they had trotted at the head of the whole caravan both to the Pole and back. There was one, stalking alone and reserved, always unsettled and unapproachable. Nothing could replace his fallen friend Fridtjof who had long found his grave in his comrades' bellies hundreds of miles away in the Barrier.

As the *Fram* set off out of the bay a fog descended and the continent where they had had so many adventures was hidden from view as they sailed away.

On Thursday 7 March the *Fram* arrived at Hobart in Tasmania, off the southern coast of Australia. Amundsen went ashore to tell the world his news.

Final Days

18 February – 21 March 1912

ON 18 FEBRUARY Scott and his remaining men reached the depot at the bottom of the Beardmore Glacier. Evans's death had been a great blow to them – and they all feared that the same could happen to them. But if they were to stand any chance of surviving the nightmare journey they had to keep moving.

At the depot they stocked up with the meagre food supplies it contained. Then they carried on to where they had shot the ponies. They dug up a carcass and ate it. It was the first time for weeks they had felt full of food.

They had expected that it would be warmer back on the Barrier but Scott noted that there was now a greater difference between the day- and night-time temperatures than before. Winter was decidedly on its way. Over the last few weeks the sun had been dipping lower and lower in the sky until it finally disappeared every day for a few hours around midnight. It would not be long before it disappeared altogether for the winter. There would be no hope for the team if they didn't reach safety by then.

Scott and his men struggled on, pulling the sledge with difficulty over the loose, sand-like snow. They were now travelling about seven miles a day, which was taking them roughly nine hours. On the way south they had been completing 15 miles or so along this stretch.

Between 26 February and 2 March the weather turned very, very cold. The minimum temperature dropped below −34 °C every day. The temperatures meant that the snow on the ground became (in the words of Scott) like *"a thin layer of woolly crystals."* The friction against the runners was terrible. It was very difficult to move the sledge – or even the skis – forward.

On 1 March Scott's team reached another depot. Here they found some of the fuel had leaked from its container – only one litre of the paraffin remained. As Amundsen had predicted, the very cold temperatures had caused the fuel to seep out at the seals. Without fuel Scott and his men would not be able to melt snow into water to add to the hard pemmican or even to boil water for tea.

Since reaching the Barrier the men had been hoping that the dog sledge was going to come out from Cape Evans to meet them. It was the one thing they discussed with any optimism. But in sending his supply teams back on the return journey, Scott had given a series of conflicting orders. Nothing had been written down so it was not clear to the Cape Evans party what they were expected to do. Unknown to Scott a dog sledge had been waiting at the Mount Hooper depot at the beginning of March with Cherry-Garrard and Demetri – but it had been unable to continue further because there was not enough food for the dogs. By the time Scott and his men staggered to Mount Hooper on 9 March, the dog team had returned to Cape Evans.

The frostbite in Oates's feet had now turned to gangrene. It took him an hour every morning to put his boots on his swollen feet. On top of this he may have been suffering from the wound he had received in the Boer War ten years previously, which had probably reopened. A shortage of Vitamin C can make scars disintegrate and cause old wounds to reappear. Oates could now only stagger in agony alongside the sledge.

Scott wrote that Oates:

> ...must know that he can never get through. He asked Wilson if he had a chance this morning, and of course Bill had to say he didn't know. In point of fact he has none. Apart from him, if he went under now I doubt whether we would get through. The weather conditions are awful, and our gear gets steadily more icy and difficult to manage. At the same time of course poor Titus is the greatest handicap... Poor chap! Poor chap. It is too pathetic to watch him.

However, Oates was not going to give up yet; he was determined to continue the journey as far as he could. He cut a slit in his sleeping bag and slept with his feet outside so the frostbite would remain frozen at night. He didn't want to cope with the terrible pain of his feet thawing and then freezing again. But by 14 March Oates knew he couldn't continue much further. His pain was agonizing, he was feeling the cold very badly, and he knew he was holding back the rest of the men.

A couple of nights later in the tent, he gave his diary to Wilson, asking him to hand it over to his mother. Scott wrote, "*Oates slept through the night ... hoping not to wake.*" But he did wake up. It was probably Oates's 32nd birthday, 17 March (Scott wrote in his diary that they had lost track of dates by now).

The wind was beating against the tent outside. Oates struggled out of his sleeping bag and pulled himself slowly across the legs of the others to the entrance of the tent. He undid the flap. "*I am just going outside and may be some time*", he said to his companions as they watched him with heavy hearts. They knew what he was probably going to do and the sacrifice he was about to make for them.

He crawled out, without his boots, into the short tent tunnel, stood up with difficulty and limped off into the surrounding snow. It was the last anyone saw of him. By now Scott was the only one keeping a diary. He wrote, "*we knew that poor Oates was walking to his death, but ... we knew it was the act of a brave man and an English gentleman.*"

The mood of the three remaining men was very sombre. They were aware how close they could be to their own deaths, but the desire for life pushed them forward. They struggled on, hauling their sledge, and by 21 March were just 11 miles from One Ton Depot – a day's journey.

They put up the tent for the night. A blizzard blew up and was there all the next day. They were very short of food and fuel, and they knew they had to move on. Scott himself could now hardly walk, he had severe frostbite in his right foot. He knew that, even if he were to reach safety, his foot would have to be amputated.

Wilson and Bowers wanted to try to go on to the depot and attempt to bring back supplies to him. Though neither of them were in good condition themselves, they felt they could get there – just.

But they didn't go.

Trapped by the storm, the three men remained in the tent, listening to the blizzard howling outside and waiting for it to die down.

On 22 March Scott wrote in his diary:

"Bad blizzard as ever – Wilson and Bowers unable to start – tomorrow last chance – no fuel and only one or two of food left – must be near the end. Have decided it shall be natural – we shall march for the depot with or without our effects and die in our tracks."

But they never left.

They wrote letters while they waited for what they knew was almost certain to be the end. Wilson and Bowers wrote some short and sad notes to members of their families. Scott, however, wrote many, many letters – to family, sponsors, contacts, the press and the public. Scott's last diary entry is 29 March:

> *Every day we have been ready to start for our depot 11 miles away, but outside the door of our tent it remains a whirling drift. I do not think we can hope for better things now. We shall stick it out to the end, but we are getting weaker, of course, and the end can not be far. It seems a pity, but I do not think I can write more ... For God's sake look after our people.*

Amundsen
Telling the World
March 1912 – June 1928

WHEN AMUNDSEN ARRIVED in Hobart, Tasmania, the first thing he did was to ask if any news had been heard of Scott's expedition. He was very relieved when he discovered that he was the first to get back to civilization. But for all he knew the *Terra Nova* could be well on her way to New Zealand – he needed to spread the word of his achievement as quickly as possible.

Amundsen refused to speak to any of the journalists that rushed to see him in Tasmania as he wanted the first news of his journey to be released through a paper in Norway. One of the disappointed journalists called him a *"dour Norse sea king"*. Amundsen sent a coded cable to his brother, Leon, in Norway:

POLE ATTAINED 14–17 DECEMBER. ALL WELL.

(In fact, Amundsen hadn't changed his calendar when crossing the International Date Line. The dates in Amundsen's journal were later changed for publication.)

He also cabled King Haakon VII.

When the news of Amundsen's success came out, via Norway, newspapers everywhere placed the story on their front pages. *"The whole world has now been discovered,"* wrote the *New York Times*. Amundsen's brother had arranged that the *Daily Chronicle* in London had exclusive first rights on the story outside Scandinavia and cabled Amundsen a coded message asking him to send something to them. The paper paid £2,000 for the story, a lot of money in those days.

Numerous cables of congratulation followed, including one from the US President, Theodore Roosevelt. Amundsen also received one from a Norwegian tinned-fish producer who wanted to put Amundsen's picture on his tins.

C

Three weeks later, on 1 April, the *Terra Nova* arrived in New Zealand. Lieutenant Evans was on board and he had news of Scott – last seen 150 miles from the Pole on 4 January. Amundsen had reached it three weeks before. The world couldn't deny that Amundsen had won the race.

Scott had sent Evans back with the message, *"I am remaining in the Antarctic for another winter in order to continue and complete my work."* Scott had also sent further writings back with the *Terra Nova*. A Norwegian paper wrote that Scott had given:

> ... the impression that the terrain and weather were much worse [than] Amundsen's. This can hardly be the case. From Amundsen's account, one can see, for example, that he was forced to lie still for four days in a snow storm. But he considers it as something that belongs to such a journey – it's "all in the day's work," and he doesn't make a fuss about it.

Amundsen began his lecture tour in Australia and then New Zealand. He also started writing a book on his travels. But a British publisher, William Heinemann, who had read Amundsen's account in the *Daily Chronicle* stated:

> *" am ... disappointed with the want of imagination he displays ... in even so thrilling a thing as his achievement ... I cannot help feeling that however great Amundsen's feat is, he is not likely to write a good book.*

Heinemann was proved right. Amundsen was not an exhibitionist and underplayed the dangers that he and his men had faced on the expedition. In his book he had made his whole trip sound too easy. He was criticized for being very unemotional.

The difference between Amundsen's and Scott's writing and reporting styles was already having an effect.

In England, although the Royal Geographical Society and others sent him cables and letters of congratulations, a feeling was growing that Amundsen had won only because he had been "lucky".

Amundsen was lecturing in America when, in February 1913, he heard the news of Scott's death. A journalist described how Amundsen:

> ...looked the picture of grief, and strove unsuccessfully to conceal his emotion ... "Horrible, horrible!" exclaimed Amundsen, as he walked back and forth ... "I cannot read that last message of Scott's without emotion ... And to think," (he added) in hushed tone, "that while those brave men were dying out there in the waste of ice, I was lecturing in warmth and comfort in Australia."

The world was shocked by the story of Scott's death. Immediately the press in England printed headlines praising Scott and stating that Amundsen was a cheat. Various reasons were cited, especially the fact that Amundsen had originally been very secretive about his intentions to go to the South Pole; and that he had used dogs and not man-hauled (*the traditional British way of crossing snow*").

Other factors were mentioned to show the difference between the two men, aiming to place Scott in a better light. The British were said to have been kind to their animals on the expedition (details of killing the ponies were not widely publicized), while the Norwegians had been cruel to have slaughtered their dogs so clinically.

The press also said that Scott's expedition had not just been about being first to the Pole but also included scientific research and was therefore far more worthy than the Norwegian enterprise.

Amundsen never seemed to receive the recognition that was his by right for reaching the South Pole first. He continued to live in Norway and to travel around the world giving lectures. He was a lonely, often solitary, man who found it difficult to make close friends. He never married.

Yet he was to achieve one final polar record. In 1926 he was part of a team that flew over the North Pole in an airship. This first flight ever over a pole also made him the first person to have seen both the North and South Poles. The pilot of the airship was an Italian called Umberto Nobile.

Two years later Amundsen heard that Nobile had gone missing on another Arctic flying trip. He secured an aeroplane and set off to look for him. The plane disappeared and he was never seen again.

Amundsen died in the Arctic, the place of his childhood dreams.

The Legend Begins

November 1912

IN NOVEMBER 1912, in the light of the next Antarctic summer, a search party set out from Cape Evans to look for Scott and his polar party. The searchers hoped to discover what had happened to them.

When Scott's tent was found by Dr Atkinson and the others, only 15 centimetres of the top pole was sticking out through the surrounding snow. Another severe blizzard might have covered it for ever and the diaries and letters of the men inside might never have been found. Then the world would never have known the fates of the men.

Scott was found lying between Wilson and Bowers with his face contorted in pain. He had obviously suffered severely from frostbite. The other two men looked more at peace.

Atkinson and Lashley entered the tent. Gran, who was standing outside, heard a crack – he later discovered it was the sound of Scott's arm breaking as Atkinson tried gently to move it to release the diaries and notes from underneath it.

Among the many letters Scott had written was one entitled "*Message to the Public*". Atkinson took it outside the tent and read it to the others:

> *We are weak, writing is difficult, but for my own sake I do not regret this journey, which has shown that Englishmen can endure hardships, help one another, and meet death with as great a fortitude as ever in the past... Had we lived I should have had a tale to tell of the hardihood, endurance, and courage of my companions which would have stirred the heart of every Englishman. These rough notes and our dead bodies must tell the tale...*

The legend of Scott the hero had begun.

The search party read, too, that the sledge was nearby and managed to uncover it. Wilson had been emphatic that the rocks the men had collected on the Beardmore Glacier should be taken back to England to be studied by geologists. Thirteen kilograms of rock samples were found on the sledge, which later led to the identification of the fossil Glossopteris, demonstrating the geological connection of Antarctica with adjacent continents. On the sledge they also found Amundsen's letter to Scott and to the King of Norway. The photographic films were there too.

The discoverers then took out the bamboo poles from the tent and let it collapse in on the bodies inside. This was to be the final resting place of Scott and his men. Atkinson read the burial service and the men sang "Onward Christian Soldiers", Scott's favourite hymn. They built a snow cairn over the tent and placed a cross made out of Gran's skis on top of it, with a note indicating who lay there and also mentioning Oates. They then left the tent to its fate.

The tent has never been seen again by any person. It now lies deep in the moving ice of the Ross Ice Shelf, with the bodies of Scott and his companions, working its way down to the sea below.

The recovery team set out to look for Oates's remains at the place he disappeared, but his body had long since been covered by snow. They found his sleeping bag – which the others had brought on with them on the sledge in case they had come across him – and also his personal bag containing his fur boots. One of these was cut through at the front, clearly indicating the amount of swelling and pain the army officer had suffered. Finally the search party erected a cross with the following inscription:

Hereabouts died a very gallant gentleman, Captain L. E. G. Oates of the Inniskilling Dragoons. In March 1912, returning from the Pole, he walked willingly to his death in a blizzard to try and save his comrades, beset by hardships.

Atkinson and his search team travelled back to Cape Evans and waited for the arrival of the *Terra Nova*. She came in January with flags flying and a table laid out for a banquet to welcome back the South Pole travellers. But on her arrival, the Captain, Lieutenant Evans, and his crew saw the prearranged sign on the beach – the polar party had died. In dismay, they took down the decorations and dismantled the banquet preparations.

It was near this beach that the men set up a cross, which still stands today in memory of the five dead men. The words inscribed on it were chosen by Cherry-Garrard:

In

MEMORIAM

Capt. R. F. Scott, R.N.

Dr E. A. Wilson, Capt. L. E. G. Oates, Ins. Drgs.,

Lt. H. R. Bowers, R.N.

Petty Officer E. Evans, R.N.

who died on their

return from the

Pole, March

1912.

To strive, to seek,

to find,

and not to

yield.

But the *Terra Nova* did bring some good news for the expedition. The ship had managed to pick up Campbell's party who had been stranded over the winter but had all, amazingly, survived. They had originally been picked up from Cape Adare by the *Terra Nova* in January 1912 and then left on Inexpressible Island to carry out a six-week sledging programme. But because of pack ice the boat couldn't pick them up at the end of February to take them to the Cape Evans base. The men had endured winter in summer clothes, with no hut, and only a month's worth of rations. They had built a snow cave and were near enough to the sea to hunt penguins and seals – they survived on their meat, and used the blubber for cooking.

The remaining men of Scott's expedition tidied up the hut at Cape Evans, closed all the windows and doors and made their way out to the *Terra Nova*. How would the rest of the world receive their tragic news?

The *Terra Nova* reached New Zealand on 10 February. Atkinson went ashore first to send off a telegram to the press. Kathleen Scott was already travelling across the globe to New Zealand to meet her returning husband. She was told the news by the captain of her ship who had received a wireless message.

When Scott's journals were edited and published they created a sensation – especially his "*Message to the Public*". He was a man who had battled against all the forces that nature and bad luck could throw at him, doing his very best in the circumstances. Then, knowing that he was soon to die, he prepared to accept his fate, proud that he had completed a great achievement for his country. He heaped praise on his brave, patriotic team, too. Scott and his men were regarded as great heroes.

Kathleen, Scott's strong-minded wife, was no doubt behind much of the publicity. She spoke of her husband as a truly heroic patriot. It was uncertain who had died last, but Kathleen always insisted that Scott had been the last to go. (However, on the back of one of Scott's letters Bowers had scribbled a final note to his mother.) The legend of Scott as tragic hero grew and the timing of his death was to ensure that it remained so for decades to come.

The news of Scott's death had reached the world in 1912. Two years later, in 1914, much of Europe was involved in the First World War. English soldiers were sent out to the front line to fight against the Germans in the trenches of northern France. Their conditions were terrible … and any day could be a man's last. He might be killed by gas, a mortar bomb, a sniper's bullet, or shot as he rushed over the top of the trench to attack the Germans.

The story of Scott's courage in the face of his death was used to try to inspire the troops and to give them some confidence. Extracts from Scott's letters and journals were read out to the English troops to encourage them to be brave for their country. They were told that an Englishman could be positive, even when everything looked terrible. Oates was particularly singled out for giving his life to help others reach safety.

When Kathleen Scott died, many letters from soldiers of the First World War were found among her possessions stating how inspiring they had found Scott's words.

Scott continued to be regarded as a great hero in England, and worldwide, for many years.

Afterword

As THE TWENTIETH CENTURY progressed, opinions about Scott's heroic status began to change. There had always been mutterings that Scott was perhaps not as great a hero and leader of men as he had been portrayed.

It was in the late 1970s that the legend of Scott was forcefully challenged. A man called Roland Huntford wrote a book in which Scott was portrayed as a bungler who never planned properly and trusted too much to luck. In contrast, Amundsen was shown as a great, forward-planning tactician.

Many people were shocked by this account, especially in England. Huntford said that Amundsen was better organized in terms of most things, including clothes, supplies, use of sledges and dogs, and his choice of suitable men to take on the expedition. He said that Amundsen's research had been more thorough and that he had used all his experience of living among the native peoples of the Arctic to great effect. He had learned dog-driving skills, followed their example of slaughtering the weaker dogs to feed to the others on a long journey, carefully measured out his supplies over the previous winter, and took men who could ski and dog-drive well. Huntford said that Amundsen had also faced danger, but he had been more sensible in how he had tackled it. In all he said that Amundsen was a much more able and organized leader of men for this type of expedition than Scott.

Scott was completely discredited by Huntford and, since then, his methods have been questioned endlessly. Should Scott have spent more time looking at the way the peoples of the Arctic lived? Couldn't he have planned the clothes for his men and the transport for his expeditions better? Should he not have given his motor sledges more thorough tests in very tough ice and snow conditions?

Scott has also been portrayed as a man of quick temper, blamed for pushing his men too hard, and for exposing them to the possibility of scurvy by not providing suitable food.

Scott has been heavily criticized too for blaming all his misfortune on bad luck, and especially on the weather conditions. But a recent book by an experienced and senior Antarctic scientist, Susan Solomon, has supported his case. She states that data recorded over the years in Antarctica shows that the very low temperatures that Scott and his small team endured on their return to the Ross Ice Shelf were extremely unusual for the particular time of the year – the temperatures are normally 15 degrees higher. This accounts, Solomon claims, for Evans and Oates suffering such severe frostbite and for the very slow progress that the man-haulers made with their sledge on the sand-paper-like, "*deadened*" snow.

After a period of nearly 100 years it is difficult to cast judgement on men who lived in a world of very different values and opportunities from today. It is probably true that Amundsen was better prepared and organized for a race to the Pole in the conditions of the Antarctic and gave himself much greater margins of safety than Scott. Amundsen transferred the traditional Arctic methods of travel to the Antarctic continent, and used them well. Scott was hoping his modern motor sledges might take a lot of the strain out of the travel for his men – but these were not to prove their worth. Yet, ironically, it is now the descendants of Scott's new-fangled motor sledges that are in daily use in Antarctica, replacing the dog teams that used to be there.

Whatever criticisms have been thrown at both men, Scott and Amundsen were both great achievers in extreme conditions – no one can take that away from either of them. Today, on the South Pole stands the aptly named Scott-Amundsen Research Station.

Members of Scott and Amundsen's Expeditions

Members of Scott's *Terra Nova* Expedition 1910

Expedition Leader
*Scott, Robert Falcon ("The Owner"): Captain, RN (Royal Navy)

Officers
Atkinson, Edward L ("Atch"): Surgeon, RN, Parasitologist
*Bowers, Henry R ("Birdie"): Lieutenant, Royal India Marines, In Charge of Stores
Campbell, Victor L A ("The Wicked Mate"): Lieutenant, RN
Evans, Edward R G R ("Teddy"): Lieutenant, RN, Second-in-Command
Levick, George Murray ("Toffer"): Surgeon, RN
*Oates, Lawrence E G ("Titus" or "Soldier"): Captain, 6th Inniskilling Dragoons, In Charge of Ponies

Scientific Staff
Cherry-Garrard, Apsley ("Cherry"): Assistant Zoologist
Day, Bernard C: Motor Sledge Engineer
Debenham, Frank ("Deb"): Geologist (Australian)
Gran, Tryggve ("Trigger"): Sub-Lieutenant, Ski Instructor (Norwegian)

Meares, Cecil H: In Charge of Dogs.

Nelson, Edward W ("Marie"): Biologist

Ponting, Herbert G ("Ponco"): Photographer and Film-maker

Priestley, Raymond E ("Ray"): Geologist

Simpson, George C ("Sunny Jim"): Meteorologist

Taylor, T Griffith ("Griff"): Geologist (Australian)

*Wilson, Edward Adrian ("Uncle Bill"): Chief of Scientific Staff, Zoologist and a Medical Doctor

Wright, Charles S ("Silas"): Physicist (Canadian)

Men

Abbott, George P: Petty Officer, RN

Archer, W W: Chief Steward, ex-RN

Browning, Frank V: Petty Officer, RN

Crean, Thomas: Petty Officer, RN

Dickason, Harry: Able Seaman, RN

*Evans, Edgar ("Taff"): Petty Officer, RN

Forde, Robert: Petty Officer, RN

Gerof, Demetri: Dog Driver (Russian)

Hooper, Frederick J: Steward, ex-RN

Keohane, Patrick: Petty Officer, RN

Lashley, William ("Lash"): Chief Stoker, RN

Omelchenko, Anton: Groom (Russian)

Thomas Clissold: Cook, ex-RN

Williamson, Thomas S: Petty Officer, RN

* Members of the final Southern Party

Members of Amundsen's *Fram* Expedition 1910

Expedition Leader
+Amundsen, Roald E G

Expedition Members
+Bjaaland, Olav: Champion Cross-country Skier
+Hanssen, Helmer: Dog Driver
+Hassel, Sverre: Dog Driver
Johansen, Hjalmar: experienced Arctic Explorer
Lindstrøm, Adolf Hendrik: Cook
Prestrud, Kristian: Lieutenant
Stubberud, Jørgen: Carpenter
+Wisting, Oscar

+ Members of final South Polar Party

(These lists do not include the ships' crew.)

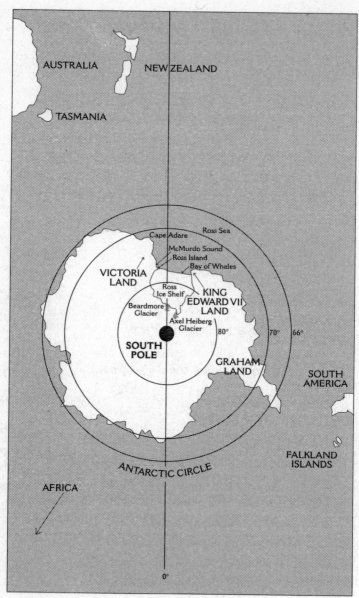

Map of Antarctica

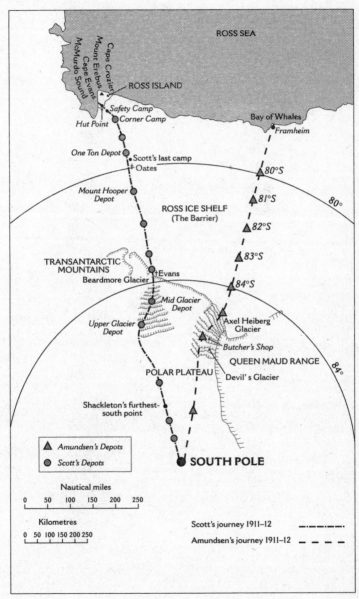

Map of Scott and Amundsen's Expeditions

Further Reading

Key books by Amundsen and Scott themselves:
The South Pole by Roald Amundsen (Cooper Square Press, 2001 – first published 1913)

Scott's Last Expedition by Captain R F Scott (John Murray, 1947 – first published 1913)

Original Film:
90° South - Herbert Ponting's black and white film of Scott's *Terra Nova* Expedition, made in Antarctica in 1910–11. This film has been recently restored and is sometimes shown at specialist cinemas, such as the National Film Theatre in London

Other books and resources used in the research included:
The Last Place on Earth by Roland Huntford (Abacus, 2000)

The Worst Journey in the World by Apsley Cherry-Garrard (Constable, 1922)

Antarctica Schools Pack by the British Antarctic Survey (Foreign & Commonwealth Office, 1999)

Scott of the Antarctic by Michael De-La-Noy (Sutton Publishing, 1997)

Scott of the Antarctic by Elspeth Huxley (Bison Books, 1990)

Scott's Last Journey edited by Peter King (Duckworth, 1999)

A First Rate Tragedy by Diana Preston (Mariner Books, 1999)

The Coldest March by Susan Solomon (Yale University Press, 2001)

Cherry: A Life of Apsley Cherry-Garrard by Sara Wheeler (Jonathan Cape, 2001)

Acknowledgements

The author would like to thank the following organizations for their assistance: Scott Polar Research Institute, British Antarctic Survey, Royal Geographical Society, and libraries in Belfast and County Down.

The author would also like to thank Peter Champion, Sally Champion, Robin Charley, Lesley Crymble, Lindsay Gowland, Brett Hannam, William Mills, Harold King and Shirley Sawtell. She would also like to thank her editor Lisa Edwards.

Picture insert

1 The *Fram* in the Bay of Whales, from *The South Pole: An Account of the Norwegian Antarctic Expedition in the "Fram", 1910-12*, Volume I, by Roald Amundsen (1872-1928) published 1912 (litho) by Norwegian School (20th century) — Private Collection/

Bridgeman Art Library (We have been unable to trace the copyright holder of this illustration and would be grateful to receive any information as to their identity.)

2 Captain Amundsen © Topham Picturepoint
3 Captain Scott writing in his journals © Topham Picturepoint
4 The "Tenements" – licensed with the permission of the Scott Polar Research Institute, University of Cambridge
5 Men getting motor sledge off the *Terra Nova* – licensed with the permission of the Scott Polar Research Institute, University of Cambridge
6 Scott and his men man-hauling sledge – licensed with the permission of the Scott Polar Research Institute, University of Cambridge
7 Wisting at the South Pole – licensed with the permission of the Scott Polar Research Institute, University of Cambridge
8 Raising the Norwegian flag at the South Pole © Mary Evans Picture Library
9 Scott and his team at the South Pole © Topham Picturepoint
10 Scott, Robert Falcon (1868-1912): last page of his diary, Antarctica, 1912 – British Museum, London, UK/Bridgeman Art Library

Index

DOUBLE TAKE
Two sides   One story

The Battle of Hastings

This is the story of the two greatest warriors of their generation, both trained in armed combat. When Edward the Confessor dies without leaving an heir to the throne of England, the two men fight for the crown in a bloody battle that will change the course of English history forever...

WILLIAM DUKE OF NORMANDY

Like his Viking ancestors, William shows a rare talent for violence and warfare. When Harold takes the crown for himself, William will amass a Norman army to stake his own claim.

HAROLD EARL OF WESSEX

Six feet tall and powerfully built, Harold is as much a man-of-action as William. He is crowned King of England, but he knows he will soon be forced to fight to keep the throne.

There are always two sides to every story...

Rivals for the crown

Two princesses, born seventeen years apart to the same father but different mothers. Their father, King Henry VIII, is determined that no woman shall ever wear the English crown. But when their younger brother, Edward, dies naming *another* woman as his successor, the two women take action – in very different ways.

MARY TUDOR

Forced by her father and brother to publicly renounce her beloved religion, Mary has a heavy cross to bear. Determined to restore England to the true Church, she decides to take matters into her own hands...

ELIZABETH TUDOR

Bright, beautiful, and highly popular at court, Protestant Elizabeth decides to lie low when Lady Jane Grey is declared queen. But must she lie even lower if Mary gets her way?

There are always two sides to every story...

Tutankhamun's TOMB

Two men share an ambition to discover a tomb that nobody else believes in. It is the burial place of a forgotten boy-king. Their search begins in a remote Egyptian valley, where fabulous treasures await them. But neither man is prepared for the consequences of opening Tutankhamun's tomb...

HOWARD CARTER

A hot-headed rising star in the field of archaeology. All his life he has dreamt of discovering the tomb of an Egyptian pharaoh, but his dream turns into a nightmare as the world's press descend on the site...

LORD CARNARVON

Wealthy and well-connected, with a passion for racehorses, fast cars and Egyptian treasures. The discovery of the tomb will be his greatest achievement, but he will pay a tragic cost...

There are always two sides to every story...